Janice VanCleave's

Ecology for Every Kid

Other Titles by Janice VanCleave

Science for Every Kid series:
Janice VanCleave's Astronomy for Every Kid
Janice VanCleave's Biology for Every Kid
Janice VanCleave's Chemistry for Every Kid
Janice VanCleave's Dinosaurs for Every Kid
Janice VanCleave's Earth Science for Every Kid
Janice VanCleave's Geography for Every Kid
Janice VanCleave's Geometry for Every Kid
Janice VanCleave's The Human Body for Every Kid
Janice VanCleave's Math for Every Kid
Janice VanCleave's Physics for Every Kid

Spectacular Science Projects series:
Janice VanCleave's Animals
Janice VanCleave's Earthquakes
Janice VanCleave's Electricity
Janice VanCleave's Gravity
Janice VanCleave's Machines
Janice VanCleave's Magnets
Janice VanCleave's Microscopes and Magnifying Lenses
Janice VanCleave's Molecules
Janice VanCleave's Volcanoes
Janice VanCleave's Weather

A+ Projects series:
A+ Projects in Biology
A+ Projects in Chemistry

Also:
Janice VanCleave's 201 Awesome, Magical, Bizarre, and Incredible Experiments
Janice VanCleave's 200 Gooey, Slippery, Slimy, Weird, and Fun Experiments

Janice VanCleave's

Ecology for Every Kid

Easy Activities that Make Learning Science Fun

John Wiley & Sons, Inc.

New York • Chichester • Brisbane • Toronto • Singapore

Illustrated by Laurel Aiello

This text is printed on acid-free paper.

Library of Congress Cataloging-in-Publication Data

VanCleave, Janice Pratt.
    [Ecology for every kid]
    Janice VanCleave's ecology for every kid : easy activities that make learning about science fun.
        p. cm.—(Janice VanCleave science for every kid series)
    Includes index.
    ISBN 0-471-10100-1 (cloth : acid-free paper).—ISBN 0-471-10086-2 (pbk. : acid-free paper)
    1. Ecology—Experiments—Juvenile literature. [1. Ecology-Experiments. 2. Habitat (Ecology) 3. Experiments.] I. Title. II. Series: VanCleave, Janice Pratt. Janice VanCleave science for every kid series.
    QH541.24.V36   1996
    574.5'078—dc20   95-6112

Printed in the United States of America

10 9 8 7 6 5

Dedicated to my grandchildren and their parents:

Calvin, Ginger, Lauren, and Laccy Russell

Russell, Ginger, Kimberly, Jennifer, and Russell David VanCleave

David, Tina, and Davin VanCleave

Acknowledgments

Many thanks to these friends and family members who are part of the present and future caretakers of our earth: Shawn Abel; Chuck, Patricia Marie, and Anthony Barth; Deborah Ann and Jessica Marie Bass; John, Jo Ann Nicole, and Aaron Michael Boutin; Jason, Caleb, Micah, and Casey Burson; John, Matthew, and Rebecca Chambers; Frances and Whitney Cooper; Phillip and Shawn Curry; Jewell and Joey Dorsey; Rachel, Rebekah, and Anna Felder; Rodney and Gary Giles; Sarah Harper; Patsy Ruth Henderson; Lynn Hinds; Meredith Husted; Dillon Taylor and Kristin Marie Kiran; Bill, Royce Carroll, Linne Trayler, Brooke Alexandra, James Andrew, Rhonda Kesler, Anthony Kaleb, Robert Logan, Judy Meador, and Jordan Breanne Johnson; Kourtney Karr; Dusty, Derek, and Drew Ladd; Gregory Lea; David Lentini; Jennifer, Kenny, and William Martin; Allison Midkiff; Kimberly and Kari Orso; Carolyne and Tommy Pasisis; Brian, Jude, and Kaitlin Patterson; Ryan and Megan Peterson; Maggie Porcher; James W. Reid V; Erica Rydholm; Jared, Sarah, and Jacob Sacchieri; Bennie Shaw; Roger, Kate, and Rebecca Bradford Scholl; Archie Robert, Norma Jo, Dianna Lynn, and Robert John Smith; Michael, Darlene Dee, and Justin Whitaker Strong; Curtis A., Vicki Marie, Julie Ann, and Cody Allen Thornton.

Contents

Introduction

Ecology is the study of the behavior of living things in their natural surroundings and how they affect each other. It is also a study of the relationships between living things and the unique home that they all share—the earth. This book explains these relationships and the consequences that can occur if any part of a relationship is disturbed or destroyed.

Understanding basic ecology can help you think about how important you are and how you affect your natural surroundings. The decisions and changes you make can have a positive effect. If you know why plants and animals live in some places and not in others, you can help **conserve** (protect from waste or destruction) wildlife. If you understand what happens to waste products, such as household garbage and unwanted chemicals from factories, you can help make the earth cleaner.

This book won't provide all the answers to ecology problems, but it will offer keys to ways that you can be a part of making the world a better place in which to live. It will guide you in discovering answers to questions relating to ecology, such as: How could killing foxes affect the number of trees in an area? When is a rose considered a weed? Is it possible that you are actually breathing air that a dinosaur may have breathed? What techniques do animals and plants use to survive the heat and lack of water in deserts?

The book is designed to teach facts, concepts, and problem-solving strategies. The scientific concepts presented can be applied to many similar situations. The exercises, experiments, and other activities were selected for their ability to be explained in basic terms with little complexity. One of the main objectives of the book is to present the *fun* of science.

How to Use This Book

Read each section slowly and follow all procedures carefully. You will learn best if each section is read in order, as there is some buildup of information as the book progresses. The format for each section is as follows:

- The chapter subtitle identifies the focus of the chapter.

- **What You Need to Know:** A definition and explanation of facts you need to understand.

- **Exercises:** To help you apply the facts you have learned.

- **Activity:** A project related to the facts represented.

- **Solutions to Exercises:** With a step-by-step explanation of the thought process.

In addition, this book contains:

- A **Glossary:** The first time a term is introduced in the book, it will be **boldfaced** and defined in the text. The term and definition are also included in the Glossary at the end of the book. Be sure to flip back to the Glossary as often as you need to, making each term part of your personal vocabulary.

General Instructions for the Exercises

1. Read the exercise carefully. If you are not sure of the answers, reread What You Need to Know for clues.

2. Check your answers against those in the Solutions and evaluate your work.

3. Do the exercise again if any of your answers are incorrect.

General Instructions for the Activities

1. Read the activity completely before starting.

2. Collect supplies. You will have less frustration and more fun if all the materials necessary for the activity are ready before you start. You lose your train of thought when you have to stop and search for supplies.

3. Do not rush through the activity. Follow each step very carefully; never skip steps, and do not add your own. Safety is of the utmost importance, and by reading each activity before starting, then following the instructions exactly, you can feel confident that no unexpected results will occur.

4. Observe. If your results are not the same as those described in the activity, carefully reread the instructions and start over from step 1.

1
Space Sharers
What Ecology Is About

What You Need to Know

The Greek word for **habitat** (the place where a plant or animal lives) is *oikos*. In 1869 Ernst Haeckel (1834–1919), a German biologist, made up the word *oekologie* to mean "the study of living things in their **environment** (the natural surroundings of living things)." Our word *ecology* is the English version of Haeckel's word, *oekologie*.

Ecologists are scientists who study organisms and their environments. **Organisms** are all living things, including people, plants, animals, bacteria, and fungi. An environment includes everything, living and nonliving, that affects an organism.

For example, an ecologist's study of the environment of a mouse in your house would include other animals of the same species, such as more mice, as well as animals of different species, which would include all family pets, you, and your family. A **species** is a group of similar and related organisms. The ecologist would also include in the study any of the mouse's **predators** (animals that hunt and kill other animals for food), such as a cat. What the mouse eats, the weather, as well as physical structures inside the house would be recorded. Fleas in the mouse's fur and bacteria inside the flea's body are also important parts of the mouse's environment. This study would give the ecologist a better understanding of why the mouse behaves in a particular way, how the mouse is affected by its environment, and how it in turn affects its environment.

MOUSE'S
ENVIRONMENT

Living organisms can be part of a larger environment and, at the same time, be the habitat for other, smaller living things. Thousands of tiny living things, such as bacteria, live inside and on the bodies of animals, including yours. Yes, your body is a habitat for other living organisms.

Unlike most animals, humans move from one environment to another throughout the day. Some of your environments are your home, school, a park, the shopping mall, and your friend's house. Another interesting thing that makes you different from other animals is that you have the ability to alter your environment. For example, in the summer you can turn on a fan or air conditioner and in the winter you can turn on a heater to change the temperature in your home.

Home

School

SOME OF
YOUR
ENVIRONMENTS

Park

Exercises

Study the figures and answer the following questions:

1. How many organisms are represented?
2. How many habitats are represented for the organisms shown?

Activity: SPREADER

Purpose   To determine how you affect the spreading of plant seeds in your environment.

Materials   8 tablespoons (120 ml) potting soil
four 5-ounce (150-ml) paper cups
masking tape
pencil
small notebook
shoe box
rubber boots

1-tablespoon (15-ml) metal measuring spoon
tap water

Procedure

NOTE: This experiment should be performed after it rains during the spring or summer.

1. Put 2 tablespoons (30 ml) of potting soil in each of the 4 cups.

2. Use the tape and pencil to label the cups 1 through 4.

3. Place the cups, pencil, and notebook in the shoe box.

4. Put on your rubber boots.

5. Carrying the shoe box, take a walk through the woods or park, and walk across a muddy area on purpose.

6. Use the spoon to scrape 1 tablespoon (15 ml) of mud from the bottom of your boots.

7. Add the mud to cup 1, and mix the mud and soil in the cup.

8. In the notebook, write a description of the area where the mud for cup 1 was collected.

9. Repeat steps 5 through 8 in a different muddy area for each of the other 3 cups, then go home.

10. With only the cups of soil and mud inside the shoe box, place the box where it will be warm and undisturbed, such as near a window.

11. Observe the contents of the cups each day for 2 weeks or until you observe plant growth. Water the soil in each cup once in a while to keep the soil moist (*not* wet).

Results   Plants will usually be found growing in some and maybe all of the cups.

Why?   The plants growing in the cups indicate that there were seeds present in the mud that stuck to your boots. Seeds from plants fall and become mixed in with the soil around them. As you walked through the mud, it stuck to the bottom of your boots. Some of the mud fell off your boots before you were able to scrape it into the cups. This fallen mud may have contained seeds. If the mud fell in an environment with the proper amount of warmth and moisture, the seeds would grow, just as the seeds in the cup grew.

You helped the plant **disperse** (spread to another location) its seeds by carrying them from one place to another on the bottom of your boots. You spread plant seeds every time you walk through an area where plants grow. This is just one of the many ways you affect your environment.

Solutions to Exercises

1. *Think!*

- Organisms are living things.

  Four organisms are represented: tree, squirrel, child, and bacteria.

2. *Think!*

- A habitat is the place where an organism lives.
- The tree is the habitat for the squirrel and bacteria.
- The house is the habitat for the boy, bacteria, and possibly the squirrel (which might live in the attic).
- The squirrel and boy are both habitats for bacteria.
- The bacteria are too small to be a habitat for any of the organisms shown.

  Four habitats are represented: tree, house, squirrel, and the boy.

2
Connections

How Plants and Animals Live with and Affect Each Other

What You Need to Know

Organisms of the same species living together in a specific area form a **population**. The term population also refers to the total count of individuals within such a group, such as the population of a town. For example, the population of Riesel, Texas, is 846, which means that 846 people live in the town.

When the populations of different species live together in the same area, they form a **community**. These organisms usually interact and depend on each other for existence.

A habitat is like an address for a species. A single habitat is the home of one species, such as interconnecting prairie dog holes. A multiple habitat is the home of many species, such as a tree where many species live. Since the different species making up a community have the same address, a habitat is also the home of a community. A desert, a lake, a single tree, a forest, or even your backyard are all habitats.

Living things cannot survive by themselves. In natural communities, each species is important to the survival of the community. The location and role or job for which a species is well suited within its community is called a **niche**. A niche includes

the species' habitat, what it eats, its activities, and its interaction with other living things.

Some niches involve many organisms. For example, a squirrel's niche could start with the squirrel's nest in a tree. The squirrel eats nuts, birds' eggs, and other organisms, and it is eaten by owls and other animals. Its waste droppings fertilize the soil, encouraging plant growth, and some of the nuts buried by the squirrel grow into new trees. These are but some of the activities that make up the squirrel's niche within its forest community.

Exercises

1. Study the figures and determine which represents a community.

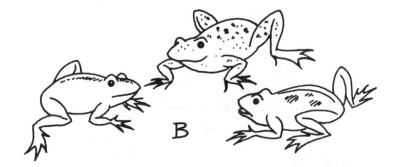

2. In the diagram, symbols are used to represent different types of species in a community. The legend explains the meaning of the symbols. Study the legend and diagram to answer the following:

    a. How many different populations are represented?

    b. Which species has the largest population?

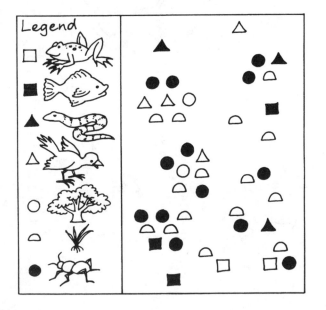

Activity: MOVERS

Purpose To determine an earthworm's niche.

Materials 2 cups (500 ml) dark-colored soil
large bowl
tap water
spoon
quart (liter) wide-mouthed jar
1 cup (250 ml) light-colored sand
1 tablespoon (15 ml) oats
10 to 12 earthworms (from a bait shop or dig your
    own)
dark-colored construction paper
rubber band

Procedure

1. Pour the soil into the bowl.

2. Slowly add water while stirring, until the soil is slightly moist.

3. Pour half of the moistened soil into the jar.

4. Pour the sand over the soil.

5. Add the remaining soil.

6. Sprinkle the oats over the soil.

7. Put the worms in the jar.

8. Wrap the paper around the jar and secure it with the rubber band. Place the jar in a cool place.

9. Every day for a week, remove the paper and observe the jar for a few minutes. Then, put the paper back over the jar and put the jar away.

10. At the end of the week, release the worms where you found them or in any outdoor garden or wooded area.

Results   The worms start wiggling and burrow into the soil. After a few days, tunnels can be seen in the soil, and the dark soil and light sand become mixed.

Why?   An earthworm's niche is very simple compared to the niches of many other organisms. The worm lives in and eats its way through the soil. It gets nourishment from the remains of other living things, especially plants, contained in the soil. The worm's movements loosen the soil so that water and air needed by plants can more easily pass through it. The worm's waste also adds to the soil nutrients that the plants need.

Solutions to Exercises

1. *Think!*

- Figure A is a single organism.
- Figure B is a group of organisms of the same species; thus, it is a population.

  Figure C is a group of different populations; thus, it is a community.

2a. *Think!*

- How many different kinds of organisms are listed in the legend?

  There are seven different populations.

b. *Think!*

- In the diagram, count the number of each symbol listed in the legend to determine the population of each species represented.

frogs	2
fish	3
snakes	3
birds	4
trees	2
grasses	15
insects	13

  Grasses make up the largest population in the diagram.

3
Togetherness

Determining Relationships between Animals of the Same Species

What You Need to Know

Most relationships between organisms have to do with working together to help everyone involved. Some of these relationships are simple and others are very complex. Small populations that live and travel together and somehow depend on each other for their well-being are called **social groups**. Many social groups function as families with equal sharing of the work. Apes have a social grouping that is similar to humans', with the young brought up in a family unit. Large populations that depend on each other are known as **colonies**.

Animals that live in colonies are called **colonial animals**. Different colonial animals show varying degrees of dependence between individuals in the colony. For example, penguins and bees are colonial animals. The major benefit to individual penguins from being in a colony is simply that there is safety in numbers. Bees, on the other hand, depend on each other in many other ways for survival and continuation of their colony.

Another type of colonial animal is the superorganism. A **superorganism** appears to be one organism but is in fact a number of colonial animals joined together. One example of a superorganism is a section of live **coral** containing thousands of tiny animals called coral polyps. Each **polyp** has a tubelike body, one end of which is attached to the sea bottom, to rocks, or to one another and the opposite end of which is a mouth surrounded by fingerlike, stinging tentacles. These flowerlike animals are linked together in such a way that food can be shared. Dead coral is the hard stony skeleton left behind when coral polyps die. Another type of superorganism is the Portuguese man-of-war. This floating balloonlike organism with dangling tentacles is actually a colony of specialized polyps, each with a specific task. This superorganism is a more effective life-form than the single organisms that it is made up of.

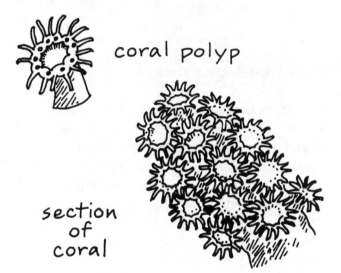

coral polyp

section
of
coral

Exercises

1. Use your imagination to design a superorganism made up of three individual organisms of the same species, each one of which performs a different job. The superorganism must be able to make food, move from one place to another, and defend itself.

2. Study each of the following figures to determine whether it represents a social group or a colony.

Activity: GLASS HOUSE

Purpose   To observe an ant colony.

Materials   2 cups (500 ml) fine soil from a flower bed, or
    potting soil
    quart (liter) wide-mouthed jar
    close-fitting gardening gloves
    long-handled mixing spoon
    cotton ball moistened with tap water
    wedge of apple
    6-by-6-inch (15-by-15-cm) square from an old
    stocking
    rubber band
    scissors
    black construction paper
    transparent tape

Procedure

CAUTION: Special care should be taken not to allow ants to get on your skin. Some people are allergic to ant stings. If you know you are allergic, do not perform this activity.

1. Pour the soil into the jar.

2. Locate an anthill outdoors and set the jar on the ground about 1 yard (1 m) from the anthill.

3. Wearing gloves, use the spoon to stir the top of the anthill. When the ants run out of the ground, scoop 2 to 3 spoonfuls of soil containing ants into the jar. You want about 15 to 30 ants in the jar.

4. Brush any ants off the outside of the jar with your gloved hand.

5. Quickly drop the moistened cotton ball and the wedge of apple into the jar. Then, immediately cover the mouth of the jar with the stocking.

6. Secure the stocking with the rubber band.

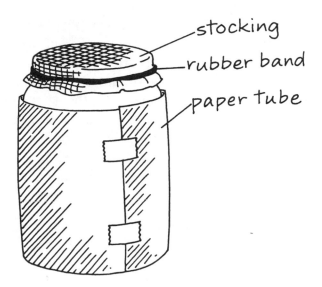

stocking

rubber band

paper tube

7. Use the scissors, paper, and tape to make a tube that fits loosely around the outside of the jar. The tube should be about 2 inches (5 cm) higher than the soil inside the jar. Place the jar in a cool place.

8. Several times a day for a week, slide the tube off the jar and observe the contents. Then, put the tube back over the jar.

9. At the end of the week, return the ants to the area where you found them by carefully shaking them out of the jar.

Results   When first placed in the jar, the ants frantically ran around, but then they settled down. Some began digging almost immediately, while others continued to explore the surface of the soil. By the end of the week, clearly defined tunnels are visible in the soil, and small anthills dot the surface. As you watch the ants move around, you may notice that each ant has a specific job.

Why?   Ants are insects that live in colonies. Each colony contains many female workers and at least one queen. A few males are produced periodically, whose only job is to **fertilize** (join a male sperm with a female egg) the queen. Queens are females that lay eggs, while workers, which make up most of the colony's population, are females that do not lay eggs. To build the tunnels where the colony lives underground, worker ants carry dirt up to the surface and dump it, creating anthills. Workers also have other jobs. Some guard the nest; some keep the nest clean; some protect the queen and the baby ants; and some gather food. You most likely collected only worker ants and could see them carrying out some of these jobs. Ants are one of just a few kinds of animals that divide up their work.

Solutions to Exercises

1. *Think!*

   • Each individual animal in the superorganism fulfills one of the three jobs: one makes food, another makes the superorganism move, and the third defends it.

   The figure is but one possible example of this imaginary superorganism.

2a. *Think!*

- A social group is a small population that lives and travels together and in some ways depends on each other.
- A colony is a large population whose members depend on each other.

The lions are a social group.

b. *Think!*

- The large number of cormorants indicate that they are not small social groups. Some seabird colonies can contain thousands of birds.

The cormorants are a colony.

c. *Think!*

- One family may live on an isolated farm, within a small community, or in a city with a million people. A larger grouping of people could be considered a colony, just as birds represent a colony.

The family is a social group.

4

Best or Worst of Friends?

Learning about Interactions between Some Closely Connected Species

What You Need to Know

In **mutualism** the relationship is between organisms of two different species in which both organisms receive some benefit. An interesting example of mutualism is that of the crocodile bird and the Nile crocodile. The crocodile allows the bird to clean its teeth and mouth. The bird picks out and eats food scraps from the crocodile's teeth, along with leeches and other organisms harmful to the crocodile. A similar relationship is that between the oxtail bird, which perches on the back of a rhinoceros and eats blood-sucking ticks and flies. All the animals benefit in these two relationships. The birds find food and the crocodile and rhinoceros are cleaned, and none of the animals are harmed.

Another example of mutualism is the relationship between the cow and the bacteria in its stomach. The cow feeds on plants, but it cannot digest the plant fiber called **cellulose** that makes up the walls of plant cells. A special cellulose-digesting bacterium found in the cow's stomach releases chemicals that

change the cellulose enough for the cow to digest it. The bacteria provide valuable nutrients to their host in return for a protected, moist, food-filled environment. Again, both organisms benefit from their relationship.

Parasitism is a relationship in which one organism, called a **parasite**, secures its nourishment by living on or inside another organism. The parasite is the **guest** and the organism that it lives on or in is the **host**. The relationship is usually beneficial to the parasite and harmful to the host. Most parasites do not kill their host. Lice and fleas are common parasites that feed off the blood of their hosts. Various kinds of worms and other organisms are common parasites that live inside animals.

Commensalism is a relationship between two organisms of different species in which the guest organism lives on or in the host organism. The guest organism benefits from the relationship, but the host is neither helped nor harmed. One example of commensalism is the **epiphyte**, a plant that grows on another plant without harming the host plant. The epiphyte receives nutrition from the air and rain instead of from its host. The host only provides a structure to cling to. Epiphytes are common in rain forests, where they live on the branches of plants to capture sunlight and rain and to receive an air supply.

Exercises

1. Use the **rebus** (pictures and symbols used to represent a word) to figure out the name of each organism described below:

    a. This organism is a bird that eats insects that live on and irritate antelopes. The bird flies up noisily when other animals approach.

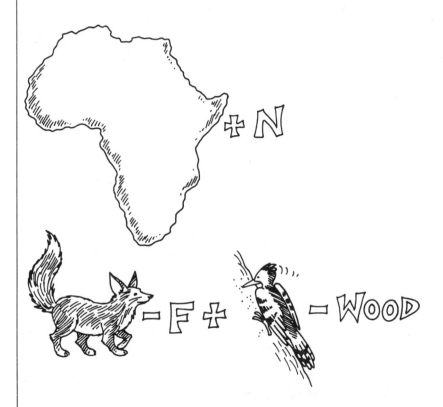

    b. This organism lives in the intestine of its host, feeding off the host's blood. The host suffers from loss of blood; it becomes thin and is easy prey to diseases.

2a. Choose one of the following words to identify the relationship between the bird and antelope described in question 1a.

- commensalism
- parasitism
- mutualism

b. Which of the words describes the relationship between the organism and its host described in question 1b?

Activity: PARTNERS

Purpose To examine a lichen.

Materials 2 or 3 samples of lichen (a pale green scaly or leafy patch generally found on the north side of trees)
desk lamp
magnifying lens

small bowl
small drinking glass
tap water
eyedropper

Procedure

1. Hold one of the lichen samples under the desk lamp.

2. Use the magnifying lens to study the entire outer surface of the lichen.

3. Place another lichen sample in the bowl.

4. Fill the glass half full with water.

5. Use the eyedropper to add 2 to 3 drops of water to the surface of the lichen in the bowl.

Results   The surface of the lichen has green and white areas. The lichen absorbs the water like a sponge.

Why? **Lichen** is a combination of green algae and a colorless fungus. Lichen is an example of mutualism. The green algae contains **chlorophyll**, a green light-absorbing pigment used in photosynthesis. **Photosynthesis** is the process by which plants use light energy trapped by chlorophyll to change a gas in the air, called **carbon dioxide**, and water into food for the plant. The algae's food is shared with the fungus, which has no chlorophyll and therefore cannot make its own food. Instead, the fungus absorbs water which contains minerals vital for it and the algae's survival. The fungus has tiny strands by which it attaches to surfaces, such as tree bark, to anchor the lichen. Both organisms benefit from their relationship.

Solutions to Exercises

1a. *Think!*

- Africa + n = African
- fox – f + woodpecker – wood = oxpecker

  The bird is an African oxpecker.

b. *Think!*

- hook + worm = hookworm

  The organism is a hookworm.

2a. *Think!*

- The African oxpecker receives nourishment from the insects that it removes from the antelope. The antelope is relieved of the irritating insects.

- The alarm the bird gives by flying up noisily prevents the antelope from being attacked by predators. Thus, the antelope lives longer and the oxpecker can continue to feed.

- Both organisms benefit from the relationship.

The relationship between the African oxpecker and the antelope is one of mutualism.

b. *Think!*

- The hookworm receives nourishment from the host's blood.
- The loss of blood harms the host.

The relationship between the hookworm and its host is one of parasitism.

5
Food Chain

How Plants and Animals Are Linked by Food

What You Need to Know

Insects eat leaves; frogs eat insects. These three organisms make up two links in a basic energy chain commonly called a food chain. A **food chain** is a series of organisms linked together in the order in which they feed on each other. Before the first link, or level, in most food chains, the primary source of energy is the sun. Plants use the sun's energy to produce their own food by photosynthesis. Thus, plants are called **producers** because they are the only organisms in the chain that can use nonliving matter to produce food.

Animals are not able to produce their own food and must eat other organisms. Thus, animals are called **consumers.** Consumers are ranked according to what they eat. If they are **herbivores** (animals that eat only plants), they are **first-order consumers. Carnivores** (animals that eat other animals) that eat first-order consumers are called **second-order consumers. Third-order consumers** eat first- and/or second-order consumers, and so forth. The organism at the top of a food chain is called the **top consumer.** There are rarely more than five levels in a food chain. Each level gets larger from top to bottom, because each organism must eat more of the organisms in the level beneath it to get enough energy to live.

FOOD CHAIN

Top Consumer

Third Order Consumer

Second Order Consumer

First Order Consumer

Primary Producer

Sun

Some bacteria and fungi cause dead plants and animals to **decompose** (to rot or decay). These organisms are known as **decomposers**. The nutrients and minerals in the decomposed material become a part of the soil. Plants feed on these nutrients and minerals from the soil. Because decomposers break down both producers and consumers to help feed the producers, they are part of the transfer of energy in the food chain. This transfer of food from the producers to the consumers to the decomposers and back again to the producers in an ongoing cycle.

Plants and animals may be food for different kinds of animals, and most animals eat more than one kind of food. Thus, many animals belong to several different food chains. The food chains in any community link together to form a **food web**. While definite food webs can be identified within each community, animals from one food web might also feed off plants and

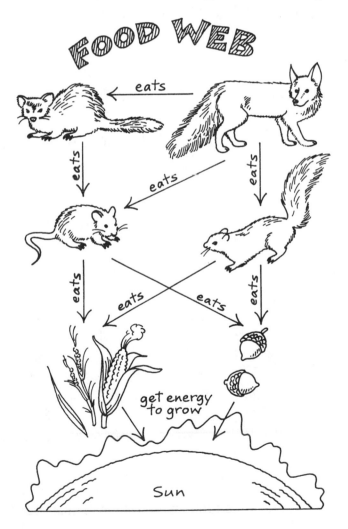

animals from another. **Omnivores** are animals that eat both plants and animals. This network of food webs creates one massive, interlinked food web composed of all life on earth.

The removal of any part of a food web could have far-reaching effects. For example, a farmer who kills too many foxes could alter the number of trees growing in that area. Without the foxes to eat the squirrels, there will be more squirrels. The squirrels will eat all the nuts from the trees. The nuts contain the seeds from which new trees grow. Because the nuts have all been eaten, no new trees will grow.

Exercises

The number of organisms in each level of a food chain varies. Use the bar graph and diagrams to answer the following:

1a. Which level of the food chain has the most organisms?

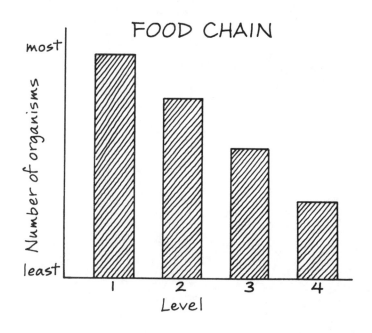

b. Which level of the food chain has the fewest organisms?

2. Which pyramid, A or B, correctly represents the number of organisms in each level of a food chain?

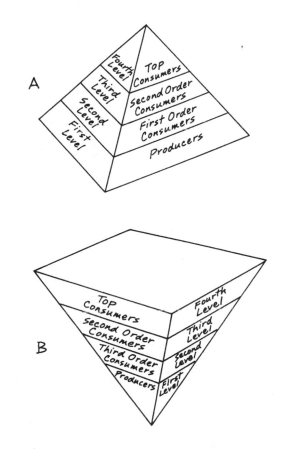

Activity: AROUND AND AROUND

Purpose   To construct a model of a food chain.

Materials   drawing compass
typing paper
scissors
pencil
18-by-8-inch (45-by-20-cm) piece of dark-colored
poster board (such as red or blue)
ruler

paper brad
transparent tape
adult helper

Procedure

1. Use the compass to draw a 7-inch (17.5-cm) -diameter circle on the paper.

2. Cut out the circle.

3. Divide the circle into three equal parts, and add the animals, plants, bacteria, and labels as in the diagram. This circle will be called the food chain wheel.

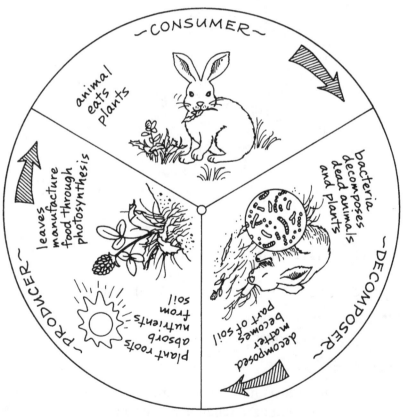

FOOD CHAIN WHEEL

4. On the poster board, measure and mark the fold lines as shown.

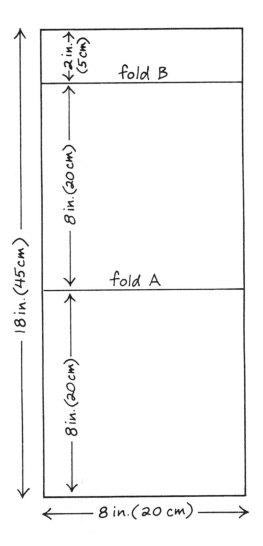

5. Fold the poster board along fold line A. The longer side of the poster board will be called the front side.

6. On the front side of the poster board, mark a dot 6 inches (15 cm) from one short edge and 4 inches (10 cm) from each long edge, as shown.

7. Draw a triangle along the fold, beginning 1 inch (2.5 cm) from each long edge and up to a point ¼ inch (0.6 cm) from the center dot.

8. Cut out the triangle through both thicknesses of poster board.

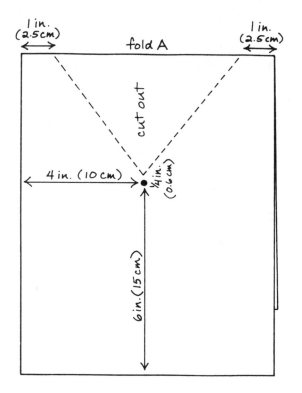

9. Have an adult use the compass to punch a hole in the center of the food chain wheel and through the center dot on the poster board. Be sure to punch the hole through both thicknesses of the poster board.

10. Insert the food chain wheel between the two thicknesses of the poster board so that the drawing faces the front side of the poster board.

11. Insert the brad through the holes in all three layers, and secure it to the back side of the poster board.

12. Fold the poster board along fold line B and secure with tape.

13. Hold the poster board with the front side facing you.

14. Turn the food chain wheel in a counterclockwise direction.

15. Observe the sequence of pictures in the triangular window.

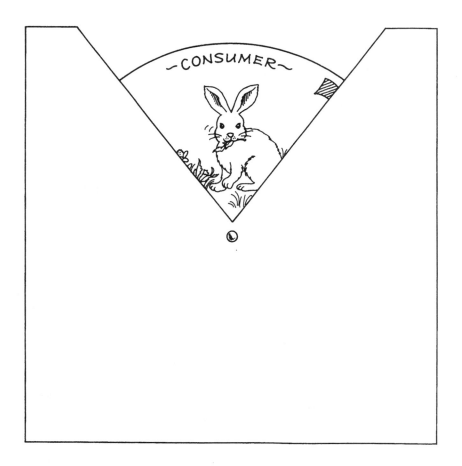

Results   A model showing the transfer of energy in a food chain is made.

Why?   One part of the food chain at a time is seen in the window. As the wheel turns, the next level in the food chain is revealed. You can follow the transfer of energy from producer to consumer to decomposer and then back again to producer.

Solutions to Exercises

1a. *Think!*

- Which level has the tallest bar on the graph?

  The first level has the most organisms.

b. *Think!*

- Which level has the shortest bar on the graph?

  The fourth level has the fewest organisms.

2. *Think!*

- The first level of a food chain is the largest, and the top, or highest, level is the smallest.
- The base (flat end) of a pyramid is the largest part, and the apex (pointed end) is the smallest.

  Pyramid A correctly represents the number of organisms in a food chain.

6
Outcasts

Discovering What a Weed Is and What Its Benefits Are

What You Need to Know

A **weed** is generally thought to be any plant that grows where it is not wanted. A pecan tree growing among orange trees is a weed if orange trees only are wanted. Even a rose is considered a weed if it is growing in a field where a farmer has planted wheat. But roses in a rose garden and pecan trees in a pecan orchard are not weeds.

While any unwanted plant is a weed, there are plants that are considered weeds no matter where they grow, such as cockleburs, nut grass, and ragweed. Plants that are not useful as food or admired for their beauty are also considered weeds. Most weeds seem to grow anywhere and need no special care. Their seeds spread easily, and weeds often grow even better than plants cared for in gardens and pastures.

It is true that weeds are generally not wanted and that much time is spent trying to get rid of them. But one good thing to be said for weeds is that they sometimes prevent **soil erosion** (the wearing away of the soil by wind or water). This is especially true where land has been cleared for the building of roads or houses. Weeds grow so easily in some areas that their roots quickly develop, holding the soil in place and keeping it from being washed away during heavy rains or blown away by the wind.

Exercise

Dandelions, bluebonnets, buttercups, and other flowering plants that grow in woods, deserts, or other natural areas are called **wildflowers**. These same flowering plants would be called weeds in a farmer's cornfield. Study the figures and identify the one that represents the sunflower as a weed.

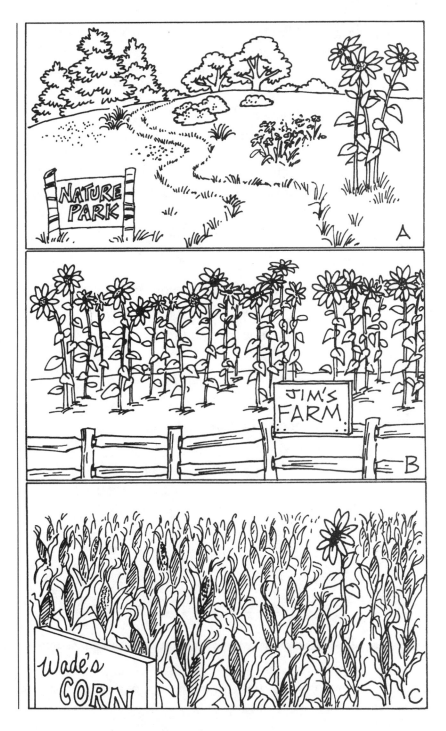

Activity: SOAKER

Purpose To show how weeds help moisten soil.

Materials ruler
masking tape
two 7-oz. (210-ml) plastic drinking cups
marking pen
potting soil
3 craft sticks
tap water
timer

Procedure

1. Place a 2-inch (5-cm) piece of tape on the side of each cup so that one end of the tape touches the rim of the cup.

2. Make a mark on the tape ½ inch (1.25 cm) from the top of the cup.

3. Pack soil into the cups up to the bottom edge of the tape.

4. Move each craft stick back and forth slightly as you insert the 3 sticks into the soil of one cup.

5. Add water up to the mark in each cup, and then mark the height again after 1 minute.

Results   The height of the water in the cup with the sticks is lower than that in the cup without the sticks.

Why?   When water is added to the cup with the sticks, the water runs into the openings the sticks make in the soil. The growing roots of weeds, or the roots of all plants, like inserting the sticks, make tiny openings as they move through the soil. This allows rainwater to fill the openings and soak into the soil instead of running over its surface. Water that soaks into the soil can be used by weeds and other plants.

Solution to Exercise

Think!

- In a nature park, flowering plants, such as the sunflower, are considered wildflowers.

- When sunflowers are grown on a farm for their seeds, which are eaten by people, they are neither wildflowers nor weeds.

- Sunflowers growing where they are not wanted, such as in a cornfield, are weeds.

  Figure C represents the sunflower as a weed.

7
Dinosaur Breath

Learning about the Oxygen Cycle

What You Need to Know

All organisms live within the earth's **biosphere** (the living part of the planet). The biosphere extends from just above to just below the earth's surface. All of an organism's needs, with the exception of energy from the sun, are supplied by the earth's resources in this layer.

If gases in the **atmosphere** (the layer of air surrounding the earth), water, and other resources vital for life were used only once, they would quickly be used up. These resources have been around and used by organisms for many years because they are **recycled** (used again). One process by which plants and animals recycle resources in the atmosphere is **respiration**. Through respiration, plants and animals take in **oxygen** (an atmospheric gas that is necessary for respiration) and give out carbon dioxide. Respiration occurs in plants and animals day and night. Photosynthesis, the process by which plants take in carbon dioxide and give out oxygen, only occurs in plants. Photosynthesis is a two-phase process. Photosynthesis–light phase requires light, so it is limited to daytime or artificial light. Photosynthesis–dark phase occurs in the absence of light.

The gases that plants give out are taken in by animals, and the gases that animals give out are taken in by plants. This recycling of gases is called the **oxygen cycle**, because oxygen or gases containing oxygen are exchanged between plants and animals. This reuse of oxygen means that you may be breathing in the same oxygen that dinosaurs breathed millions of years ago.

OXYGEN CYCLE

Exercises

1. Which of the diagrams on the next page describes the following processes:

a. photosynthesis–light phase

b. respiration

2. The diagram has four arrows, but only two of them correctly represent the oxygen cycle. Identify the two arrows.

Legend:
carbon dioxide □
oxygen ○

Activity: HOME ALONE

Purpose To demonstrate how plants can live without animals.

Materials 1 cup (250 ml) potting soil
quart (liter) jar, with lid
trowel
clump of grass
tap water

Procedure

1. Pour the soil into the jar.

2. With permission, use the trowel to dig up a clump of grass that will fit inside the jar.

3. Moisten the soil with water so that it is damp but not too wet.

4. Secure the lid on the jar.

5. Place the jar near a window but not in direct sunlight.

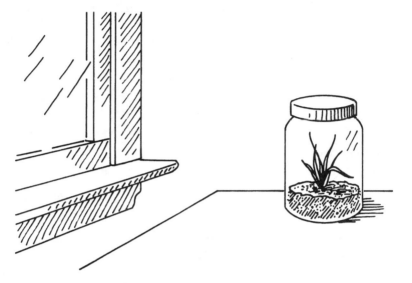

6. Observe the jar during the daytime and nighttime as often as possible for 2 weeks.

Results The inside of the jar appears cloudy at times during the daytime. Water droplets appear on the inside of the glass during the nighttime and parts of the day.

Why? Photosynthesis is the process by which chlorophyll in plants captures light energy and uses it to change carbon dioxide and water into sugar and oxygen. The sugar is used by the plant as food, and the oxygen is released into the atmosphere. Photosynthesis can be summarized as follows:

$$\text{carbon dioxide + water} \xrightarrow[\text{chlorophyll}]{\text{light energy}} \text{sugar + oxygen}$$

During the respiration process, sugar combines with oxygen to form water, carbon dioxide, and energy. Light is not needed for plant respiration. The water and carbon dioxide are released from the plant, and the energy is used by the plant to perform its life activities. Respiration can be summarized as follows:

sugar + oxygen $\longrightarrow$ carbon dioxide + water + energy

Note that respiration produces carbon dioxide and water needed for photosynthesis. The cloudiness and water droplets on the inside of the jar are partly due to water from respiration leaving the plant. Water also **evaporates** (changes from a liquid to a gas as a result of being heated) from the soil and then **condenses** (changes from a gas to a liquid as a result of being cooled). The water that results from this process is called **condensation**. It also produces droplets and cloudiness inside the jar.

The grass survives in the jar because plants make many of the materials that they need for survival. Plants can live without animals, but animals cannot live without plants because animals cannot make oxygen or produce their own food. If all the plants on the earth were destroyed, oxygen would be used up and the animals would die unless a way was found to replace the oxygen and food produced by plants.

Solutions to Exercises

1a. *Think!*

- Photosynthesis–light phase occurs when the plant is in light.
- During photosynthesis–light phase, plants take in carbon dioxide and give out oxygen.

  Diagram C represents photosynthesis–light phase.

b. *Think!*

- Respiration occurs during the daytime and nighttime in plants and animals.

- During respiration, plants and animals take in oxygen and give out carbon dioxide.

  Diagrams A and D represent respiration.

2. **Think!**

   - Animals take in oxygen that is given out by plants. Plants take in carbon dioxide that is given out by animals.

   Arrows B and D correctly represent the oxygen cycle.

8
Up and Down

Learning about the Water Cycle

What You Need to Know

All living organisms need water. In fact, life as we know it could not exist without water. Water in the earth's biosphere is used and reused again and again. This recycling is called the **water cycle**. It is the continuous movement of water between the earth and the atmosphere. The diagram on the next page shows the movement of water and how it changes during the water cycle.

One of the changes in the water cycle is evaporation, which is the changing of water from a liquid to a gas state called **water vapor**. After swimming, your wet bathing suit and skin quickly dry when you stand in the sun due to evaporation. As shown, in the diagram of the water cycle, water is always evaporating from lakes, streams, and rivers.

The leaves of plants also release water vapor into the atmosphere by a process called **transpiration**. Plant roots collect water from the soil, and the water spreads throughout the plant. Much of this water is then lost through the leaves by transpiration.

Once in the atmosphere, water vapor may be cooled and changed back into liquid water as a result of condensation. Clouds form when water vapor condenses in the atmosphere.

The water that collects on the outside of a cold soda can is also an example of condensation.

When the water droplets in clouds become large enough, they fall as **precipitation** (water that returns to the earth as rain, snow, sleet, or hail). The water falls into open bodies of water and onto the land. Some of the water that falls onto the land makes its way to open bodies of water because it runs downhill into streams that drain into lakes, rivers, and oceans. Water also soaks into the ground, where it is used by plants, evaporates, or moves underground back to an open body of water.

This back-and-forth change of water from a liquid to a gas in the water cycle continues day in and day out. In the **desert**, the amount of water that evaporates is greater than the precipitation. The reverse is true in a **tropical rain forest**. The amount of water leaving and returning to the earth may vary from place to place. However, if you consider the entire earth, the water cycle is balanced. This means that water never goes away, it just changes from one form to another.

Exercises

In the following equations, $\rightarrow$ = produces, S = solid or frozen water, L = liquid water, and V = water vapor.

    A. L – energy $\rightarrow$ S

    B. L + energy $\rightarrow$ V

    C. V – energy $\rightarrow$ L

    D. S + energy $\rightarrow$ L

Name the letter of the equation that represents the following:

1. Evaporation of water

2. Condensation of water

Activity: DRIPPER

Purpose To demonstrate the water cycle.

Materials tap water
ruler
transparent storage box about the size of a shoe
   box
plastic wrap
ice cube
resealable plastic bag
timer

Procedure

1. Pour 1 inch (2.5 cm) of water into the box.

2. Cover the top of the box with plastic wrap.

3. Put the ice cube in the bag and seal the bag.

4. Place the bag in the center of the plastic wrap that covers the box.

5. Gently push the ice down about 1 inch (2.5 cm) so that the plastic wrap slopes down toward the center.

6. Set the box near a window so that the sunlight shines on the box.

7. Observe the surface of the plastic directly under the ice cube every 20 minutes for 1 hour or until the ice melts.

Results   Water droplets form on the underside of the plastic under the ice. Some of these water droplets fall back into the water in the box.

Why?   The heat from the sun provides energy, causing some of the liquid water in the box to evaporate. The water vapor rises and condenses on the underside of the plastic, which has been cooled by the ice. As more water collects on the plastic, the droplets increase in size until their weight causes them to fall back into the water below. This is a model of the water cycle on the earth. The bottom of the box represents the surface of the earth, and the plastic represents the earth's atmosphere. As long as the box remains closed, the amount of water in the box remains the same; it just changes from one form to another.

Solutions to Exercises

1. *Think!*

- The equation for the evaporation of water reads: liquid water plus energy produces water vapor.

  Equation B represents evaporation of water.

2. *Think!*

- The equation for the condensation of water reads: water vapor minus energy produces liquid water.

  Equation C represents condensation of water.

9
Fitting In

Looking at How Organisms Adapt to Their Environments

What You Need to Know

Organisms live in many different environments. They survive when their needs for food, shelter, and protection are met. Organisms that survive have adapted to their surroundings. An **adaptation** is a physical characteristic or behavior that allows an organism to adjust to the conditions of a particular environment. For example, the feet of some animals that live in and near the water have thin skin stretched between their toes. Webbed feet enable the animal to move quickly through the water.

A desert is a land area that receives less than 10 inches (25 cm) of rainfall a year, and loses more water through evaporation than it gains from precipitation. Animals and plants of the desert have physical adaptations to store water or food or to cool off rapidly. One animal that can survive in the desert is the camel, which is able to drink large amounts of water at a single time. Another desert animal is the North American jackrabbit, which has long ears containing many blood vessels near the surface that speed the release of body heat.

The spines on cacti and some other desert plants interrupt the flow of the wind and thus help to keep the plant from drying out. If the spines are shiny, they reflect some of the sun's rays

away from the plant. Even though the spines are small, their shadows may add further protection from the sun. Spines of some cacti point downward and act as tips to concentrate light rain or heavy dew into droplets of water, which fall to the ground below the cactus. The stems and leaves of cacti are generally thick and/or round to keep the plants from losing too much water to transpiration.

Unlike other animals, you can adapt to almost any environment, from the snow-covered mountains of Colorado to the sunny beaches of Florida. This flexible adaptation is partially due to your ability to change outer clothing and footwear. Specially designed clothing to hold in body temperature would better adapt you to a snowy environment, and skis would make it easier to move on the snow. Fewer and lighter clothes would allow body heat to escape and thus keep the body cooler in a hot environment. Sandals would keep your feet cool yet protect them from hot surfaces.

You can even regulate the temperature inside your home or car by turning on a heater to warm it up or an air conditioner to cool it down. Other animals don't seem to have the mental capabilities to create clothes for different environments or to develop technology to alter or change their environments. For all other animals, and plants as well, only those that have adaptive characteristics for an environment are likely to survive.

Exercise

The organisms in the following three figures have been mislocated. Match each organism with the environment for which it is best adapted.

Activity: DIGGER

Purpose To simulate a woodpecker's special adaptation for obtaining food.

Materials raisin cookie
paper plate
pen
round toothpick

Procedure

CAUTION: Do not eat the food materials in this experiment.

1. Place the cookie on the plate.

2. Use the pointed end of the pen to dig out the parts of the cookie from around one of the raisins.

3. Use the toothpick to spear the raisin and remove it from the cookie.

Results   The pen's point breaks away pieces of the cookie from around the raisin. The toothpick easily sticks into the raisin, allowing you to remove it from the cookie.

Why?   The pen represents the strong chisel-like bill of the woodpecker, which is used to dig insects out of wood. The toothpick represents the woodpecker's lance-like tongue, which is used to spear the exposed insects.

The bill and tongue of the woodpecker are special physical adaptations of this bird. Birds that live in different environments have their own special physical adaptations for securing food.

For example, the pelican has a large dipper-shaped bill to scoop fish from the water. The pelican cannot dig insects out of trees, and the woodpecker cannot scoop fish from the water. Each is adapted to its own environment.

Solution to Exercise

Think!

- Fish have gills that allow them to breathe underwater.

  The best environment for organism 1 is C.

Think!

- Cacti do not need a lot of water.

  The best environment for organism 2 is A.

Think!

- Monkeys have tails that help them move through trees.

  The best environment for organism 3 is B.

10
Boundaries

Understanding Ecosystems and Biomes

What You Need to Know

An **ecosystem** is a distinct area that combines **biotic** (living) communities and the **abiotic** (nonliving) environments with which they interact. Biotic communities include all living organisms within the ecosystem. These organisms interact with each other as well as with the abiotic environment. The abiotic environment includes things such as sunlight, soil, moisture, nutrients, temperature, and the like. The area where two or more ecosystems merge is called an **ecotone**. There may be animals and plants from several ecosystems in this area.

The **climate** (weather over an extended period of time) of an area determines the types of plants that can live there. An ecosystem that covers a large geographic area where plants of one type live due to the specific climate in the area is called a **biome**. Each biome is identified by its **flora** (all the plants in a particular area) and **fauna** (all the animals in a particular area). The earth is divided into land biomes described by five main categories of **vegetation** (plant life). These basic biomes are briefly described as follows:

1. **Tundra:** A treeless biome mainly in the north polar areas, with long frigid winters and brief summers. Grasses, mosses, lichen, low shrubs, and a few flowering plants survive here.

2. **Forest:** A forest contains a large group of trees that usually grow close enough together that many of their tops touch or overlap, shading the ground. Forests are the most common type of vegetation and require the most rainfall.

3. **Grassland:** The main vegetation is grass or grasslike plants. Savannas are grasslands with few or scattered trees. In excessively dry areas, the grass grows in clumps called steppe grass and has bare ground between the grass clumps. In wetter areas, the grass may be 3 to 6 feet (1 to 2 m) tall.

4. **Desert:** A desert is a biome with less than 10 inches (25 cm) of rainfall each year. Some deserts have little or no vegetation, while others have **scrub** (small trees and shrubs) and grassy patches. Desert plants have different ways of adapting to the dry climate. Some, such as cactus, store water for long periods of time; others remain **dormant** (inactive) in seed form until enough rain falls.

5. **Mountain:** A mountain is a biome of high ground with various types of vegetation depending on the elevation. A single mountain may start with a desert at the base, change into forest, then become grassland, and end in a tundra at the top.

Water ecosystems include freshwater plants in and around rivers and lakes as well as saltwater plants in and around oceans. Oceans make up the largest ecosystem, since they are all linked together.

All the ecosystems combined make up the earth's biosphere. The biosphere covers the whole surface of the earth and is the part of the earth where life exists. *Bios* comes from a Greek word meaning "life." The biosphere extends about 10,000 yards (9,000 m) above the surface of the earth at **sea level** (the level of the surface of the ocean) and about 500 yards (450 m) below the earth's surface. The earth is the only planet known to have a biosphere.

BIOME VEGETATION REGIONS

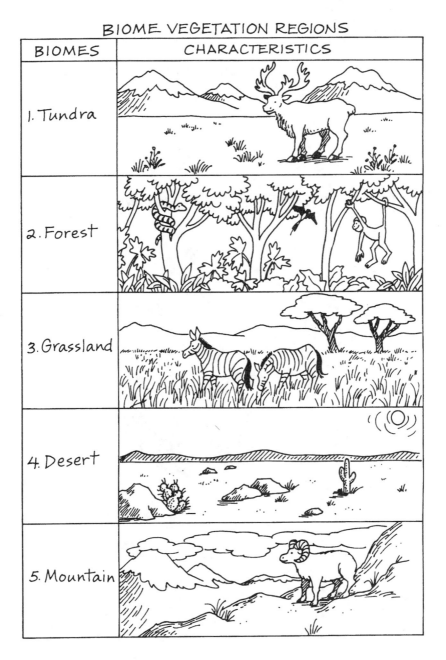

BIOMES	CHARACTERISTICS
1. Tundra	
2. Forest	
3. Grassland	
4. Desert	
5. Mountain	

Exercises

1. Use the Biomes of Australia map to determine the locations of the following types of biome:

   a. desert

   b. forest

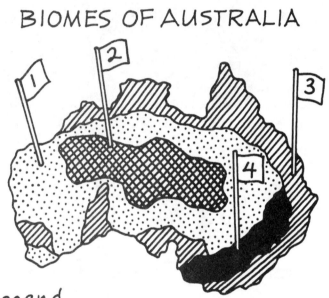

BIOMES OF AUSTRALIA

Legend

▨ little or no vegetation

▨ grass and grasslike plants

▨ broadleaf trees

▨ broadleaf and needleleaf trees

2. Match each biome with the figure that correctly represents it.

    a. forest

    b. grassland

    c. desert

Activity: SAMPLER

Purpose   To study a section of an ecosystem.

Materials   measuring tape
　　　　　9 sharpened pencils
　　　　　70 feet (21 m) of cord
　　　　　graph paper
　　　　　marking pen
　　　　　compass
　　　　　thermometer

Procedure

1. Select a study area that has a variety of plant life. This can be a forest, an open field, or the yard around your home.

2. With the measuring tape, measure an area 10 × 10 feet (3 × 3 m).

3. At each of the four corners of the plot, drive a pencil into the ground, leaving about 5 inches (12.5 cm) of the pencil above ground.

4. Use the measuring tape to divide each side of the plot into 5-foot (1.5-m) sections.

5. Drive a pencil into the ground at each 5-foot (1.5-m) interval along all sides of the plot. Drive a pencil into the ground at the center of the plot.

6. Using cord to join adjacent (neighboring) pencils, divide the plot into four equal subplots.

7. On graph paper, sketch the plot. Identify each subplot with a number. Indicate the compass directions (N, S, E, and W) with arrows on the sketch.

8. Make a sketch of each subplot. Note the number and size of prominent features, such as rocks, trees, trails, open areas, erosion, animals, and the like.

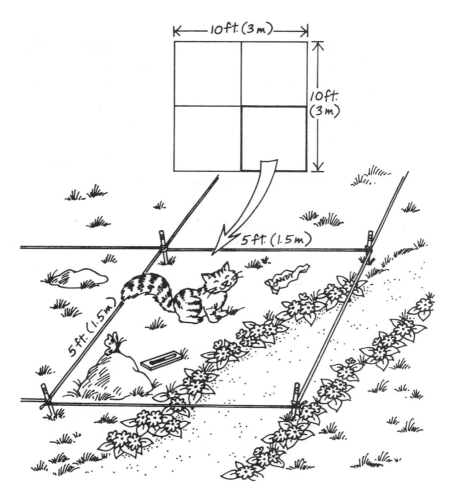

9. Use the thermometer to determine the temperature in different locations of each subplot.

Results   A plot of ground is selected, measured, and subdivided as a sample ecosystem. A general description of the number and size of prominent features in each subplot is noted.

Why?   The subplot allows you to study biotic features (plants, animals, and insects) and abiotic features (soil, walkways, rocks, litter, temperature, and the like). In this study, the number as well as the size of both abiotic and biotic features can be taken. Separate information taken from each subplot, when studied as a whole, provides a clear picture of the **ecological community** (interaction of living organisms with their environment) within the plot. This information gives you clues to the surrounding ecosystem. However, for more valid information you must follow the example of ecologists and study more plots. These plots should be selected randomly from different locations within the ecosystem.

Solutions to Exercises

1a. *Think!*

- Deserts have little or no vegetation.

  Section 2 is a desert.

b. *Think!*

- Forests contain trees.

  Sections 3 and 4 are forests.

2a. *Think!*

- The main characteristic of a forest is that it has a large number of trees.

  Figure B is a forest.

b. *Think!*

- The main characteristic of a grassland is that it is grassy.

  Figure A is a grassland.

c. *Think!*

- A desert has little vegetation. A cactus is a desert plant. *Figure C is a desert.*

11
Icy Lands

Learning about Plants and Animals in Polar and Tundra Biomes

What You Need to Know

The earth is divided in half north and south by an imaginary boundary called the **equator**. The area of the earth above the equator is called the **Northern Hemisphere**, and the area below the equator is the **Southern Hemisphere**. The **Arctic Circle** is the imaginary boundary of the northern polar region

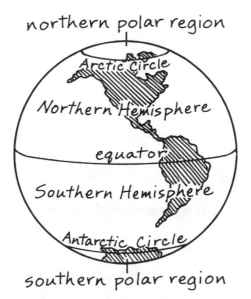

in the Northern Hemisphere, and the **Antarctic Circle** is the imaginary boundary of the southern polar region in the Southern Hemisphere.

In the polar regions, it is freezing cold and the land and water are covered with ice year-round. This harsh climate is too cold to support most plant life; however, researchers have found a few species of moss and lichen in the Antarctic.

Tundra biomes are found mostly north of the Arctic Circle. While winters in a tundra can be long, there is a brief, intense growing season because of very long daylight hours in the summer. The tundra soils are frozen for most of the year, but melting ice provides the moisture needed for plant growth. There are no tall plants, but grasses, lichens, mosses, low shrubs, and a few flowering plants can survive in this harsh environment. Because these plants are low to the ground, they are protected from the strong, cold winds coming from the polar regions.

An important feature of a tundra is **permafrost** (a layer of permanently frozen soil underground). During the warming season, the top layer of the soil thaws, but the layers below, or subsoil, remain frozen. Plants must quickly go through their cycle of growth and reproduction before the top layer freezes again. Some plants go from seed through germination, growth, flowering, and seed production in as little as 40 days.

Animals in a tundra **hibernate** (spend the winter in a sleeplike condition of partial or total inactivity), **migrate** (move from one place to another), or live under the snow. Some of the animals found in this area are caribou, foxes, hares, lemmings, musk oxen, and wolves. Most birds come during the short warm period to reproduce and then migrate to warmer areas for the remainder of the year.

Exercises

1. Study the map and answer the following:

   a. Where is the largest area of tundra?

   b. Where is the largest area of ice-covered land?

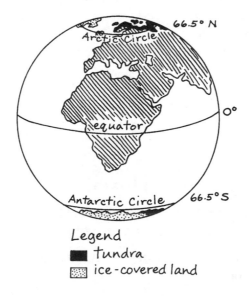

2. Which of the figures represent vegetation that might be found on a tundra?

Activity: BRRRRR!

Purpose To determine how skin covering protects animals from the cold.

Materials 5 to 6 ice cubes
large bowl
tap water
thermometer
timer
paper towel
wool glove
plastic bag

Procedure

1. Place the ice cubes in the bowl and fill the bowl with water.

2. Allow the thermometer to sit for 10 minutes so that it records the correct temperature of the air in the room.

3. Hold the thermometer in your hand and place your thumb over the bulb.

4. Gently press your thumb against the bulb for 5 seconds.

CAUTION: Do not press too hard. The glass bulb could break.

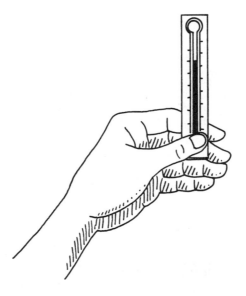

5. Observe the change in the temperature reading as you hold the bulb.

6. Place the same hand in the bowl of ice water for 5 seconds.

7. Dry your hand with the paper towel. Immediately hold the thermometer in your chilled hand and press your thumb against the bulb for 5 seconds.

8. Observe the change in the temperature reading.

9. Repeat steps 3 through 6, wearing the wool glove. Place your gloved hand inside the plastic bag for step 6 to keep the glove from getting wet.

10. Remove the bag and glove from your hand. Immediately hold the thermometer in your chilled hand and press your thumb against the bulb for 5 seconds.

Results Holding the thermometer with your hand at normal body temperature causes the reading to increase. The thermometer reading decreases when the bulb is pressed by your chilled hand. The chilled gloved hand stays warmer than the chilled hand without the glove.

Why? Heat energy moves from warmer objects to cooler objects. A thermometer indicates whether an object is giving out heat or taking in heat. At the beginning of the experiment, your thumb is at its normal body temperature of about 98.6 degrees Fahrenheit (37°C). Body temperature is usually greater than room temperature, so the thermometer reading should increase when you hold your warm hand against the bulb. The second, lower reading indicates that, after being placed in ice water, your skin has lost heat energy and is cooler than normal body temperature. The wool glove acts as an **insulator** (a material that does not easily gain or lose energy) in that it keeps the heat of your hand from being lost to the cold water. The insulating glove keeps your hand warmer, just as insulating fur and feathers on animals keep their skin warmer.

Solutions to Exercises

1a. *Think!*

- What is the symbol for tundra on the map? Solid areas.

  The largest area of tundra is above the Arctic Circle, or latitude 66.5° north of the equator (66.5°N).

b. *Think!*

- What is the symbol for ice-covered land on the map? Dotted areas.

  The largest area of ice-covered land is below the Antarctic Circle, or latitude 66.5° south of the equator (66.5°S).

2. *Think!*

- There are no tall trees on a tundra.

  Figure B represents vegetation that might be found on a tundra.

12
Woodlands
Learning about Plants and Animals in Forest Biomes

What You Need to Know

There are three basic types of forest: coniferous, deciduous, and tropical rain forest. **Coniferous forests** contain **coniferous plants** (plants whose seeds are produced in cones), which typically have needles instead of leaves. Most conifers are **evergreens** (plants whose needles or leaves remain green throughout the year). This type of forest exists where winters are very cold and long and there is low rainfall, such as in the northern parts of North America, Europe, and Asia, and in the world's mountain regions. These forests form a strip south of the tundra in the Northern Hemisphere. A coniferous forest is sometimes called a boreal forest (after the Greek name for the north wind), northern coniferous forest, or taiga.

Deciduous forests contain **deciduous plants,** which shed their leaves once a year and are usually found in areas with mild temperatures and abundant rainfall throughout the year. These forests can be found in Japan, most European countries, and in Asia and North America.

Tropical rain forests are located between the Tropic of Capricorn (latitude 23.5°S) and the Tropic of Cancer (latitude 23.5°N). The temperature in most rain forests varies little during the year, averaging between 70 degrees and 85 degrees Fahrenheit (21° and 29°C). These warm temperatures and a rainfall of more than 80 inches (200 cm) a year make rain forests very humid. This warm, moist environment results in many different kinds of plants and animals.

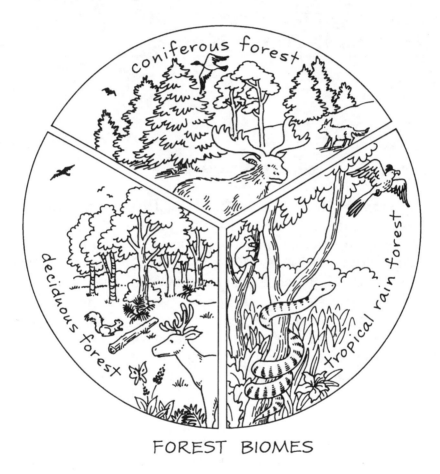

FOREST BIOMES

Life in the different forests varies due to the differences in climate, but all forests are alike in that they are several communities in one. Forests are made up of different layers, the number of which depends on climate, soil, age, and other things, such as whether trees are cut for lumber. The following is a brief description of the six basic forest layers:

1. **Emergent layer:** This is the tops of the tallest trees, which may rise 30 feet (10 m) or more above all the other trees in the forest. Because these trees stick out above the others, they often endure changing temperatures and strong winds.

2. **Canopy layer:** This is the roof of the forest. It is a network of branches and leaves that forms a covering that blocks some of the sunlight from lower plants.

3. **Subcanopy layer:** Under the canopy layer are shorter trees. Many of these trees are adapted to growing in the shade and will remain short, but some will take the place of larger trees that have died and fallen. The fallen trees provide an opening for sunlight to come through as well as space in which another tree can grow.

4. **Shrub layer:** Under the subcanopy layer are the shrubs. Shrubs are shorter than trees and usually have many stems instead of one main branch.

5. **Herb layer:** Plants that grow close to the ground, such as flowers, grasses, ferns, and seedlings, form this layer.

6. **Floor layer:** This is the bottom layer of the forest. It is made up of lichens and mosses, which grow in the remains of fallen trees, branches, and leaves.

Each layer of the forest has its own special community of plants and animals. Forest animals build their homes, feed, and carry out most of their activities mainly in one or two layers of the forest. Each animal species finds what it needs to survive in a particular layer. Many floor animals never rise above the floor level, and while birds in the emergent layer may swoop down to the forest floor for food, they usually bring it back to their nests in the emergent layer.

Exercises

1. Study the figure and identify the area where these forest organisms live.

    a. Harpy eagles build nests in the tallest trees, from which they watch alertly for animals on which they feed.

    b. Termites (wood-eating insects) are found in dead trees.

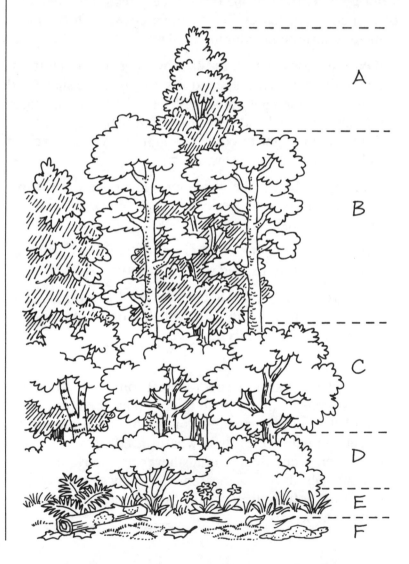

2. Epiphytes are plants that grow on other plants without harming them. They need sunlight and receive nourishment from rain and air. Study the figure and identify the area where epiphytes are least likely to be found.

Activity: GLIDER

Purpose To make a model of a flying squirrel.

Materials brown crayon
typing paper
black marking pen
large paper clip

Procedure

1. Color one side of the paper brown.

2. Lay the paper on a table, brown side up.

3. Fold the paper in half lengthwise twice.

4. Unfold the paper and lay it on a table, white side up. Label the fold lines A, B, and C.

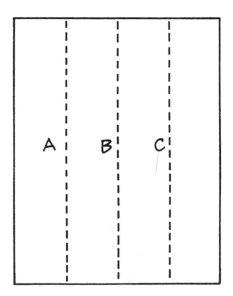

5. Fold the paper so that the top corners of the paper meet at
the center fold line B. The point at the end of fold line B
will be called point D.

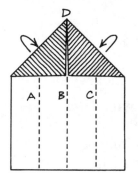

6. Turn the paper over and refold along fold line B. Lay the
paper on the table so that fold line B is to the right.

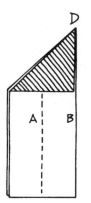

7. Fold point D down so that it meets fold line A.

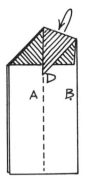

8. Refold only the faceup side of the paper along fold line A. With the pen, draw a flying squirrel on the paper as shown.

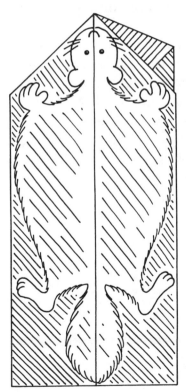

9. Attach the paper clip to the underside as shown.

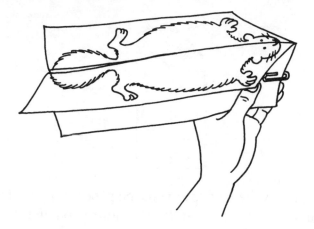

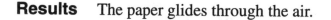

Results   The paper glides through the air.

Why?   As the paper moves forward, air flowing over the outstretched wings lifts the paper, allowing it to glide. Flying squirrels, like the paper model, glide rather than fly. They have special flaps of skin that extend from their front legs to their hind legs. When the squirrel leaps from one branch to another, the skin is stretched out like sails to help it glide. Flying squirrels are found in the forests of North America, Europe, Asia, and Africa.

Solutions to Exercises

1a. *Think!*

- The tallest trees are in the emergent layer.

  Harpy eagles live in layer A.

b. *Think!*

- Most dead trees are found on the floor of the forest.

  Termites are most likely to be found in layer F.

2. *Think!*

- Epiphytes do not grow in the ground.
- Epiphytes need light. Which layer has the least amount of sunlight?

  Epiphytes are least likely to be found in layer F.

13

Grasslands

Learning about Plants and Animals in Grassland Biomes

What You Need to Know

Grasslands, a major biome of the Earth, are **semiarid**, which means the climate is dry, but not as dry as a desert. Grasslands get 10 to 20 inches (25 to 50 cm) of rain per year. This climate is too dry for most trees to grow, but grasses or grasslike plants do well here. The few trees and shrubs that do live in grasslands are usually found along streams or in low areas where there is more moisture.

Grasslands are mostly flat with some rolling areas. They exist in the tropical zone and northern and southern temperate zones. The **tropical zone** is the region between latitudes 23.5°N and 23.5°S. The **northern temperate zone** is the region between latitudes 23.5°N and 66.5°N. The **southern temperate zone** is the region between latitudes 23.5°S and 66.5°S. Temperate grasslands have distinct hot and cold seasons. The winters can be very cold and the summers hot and dry. Tropical grasslands have year-round high temperatures and a long dry season in summer. Because of the dryness of all grasslands, periodic fires commonly spread across them and temporarily rid the area of shrubs and trees. The grasses survive the heat and regrow, because a large amount of the growing parts of grasses is below ground.

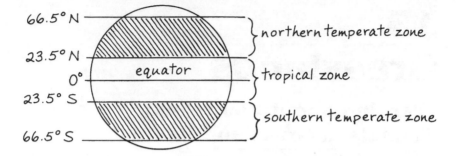

Grasslands across the earth support a large variety of wildlife, including many grazing hoofed animals, such as wildebeests, gazelles, impalas, zebras, and antelope. These animals trample grass seeds into the ground and fertilize the soil with their droppings, which helps the grass grow. Burrowing animals, such as ground squirrels and rodents, live underground, where they are safe from predators and fires. Their burrowing also helps break and mix up the soil, which helps the soil absorb water and thus helps the grasses and other plants grow. Besides these herbivores, a large variety of carnivores live in grasslands.

All grassland organisms are adapted to distinct wet and dry seasons, including prolonged **droughts** (extended periods of unusually low rainfall). Some of the plants become dormant in the dry season and resume their growth when it rains. Some develop long roots that can find water at greater depths. Most animals migrate to find food and water during dry periods, returning with the rains that restore the land with life.

Ecologist's Toolbox: Guide to Grass-Eaters

Materials   ruler
           scissors
           typing paper
           marking pen

Procedure

1. Measure the Tropical Grassland Grass-Eaters chart, then cut a piece of paper that is the same length but twice as wide as the chart.

2. Fold the paper in half lengthwise.

3. Unfold the paper, then fold it in half widthwise (from top to bottom) twice.

4. Unfold the paper, then use the ruler and pen to draw a line across the paper along each of the three fold lines made in step 3. Make the lines dashed on the left side of the length-wise center fold and solid on the right side of this fold.

5. Add the label "Guide to Grass-Eaters," number the three sections above this label, and draw a grass plant on the right side of the center fold as shown.

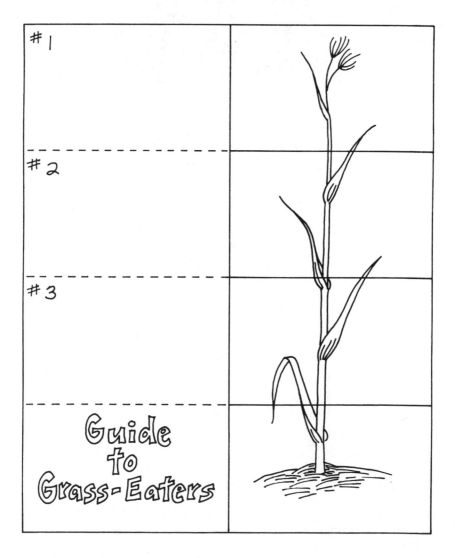

6. Cut along the dashed lines so that each numbered section becomes a flap.

Exercise

The tropical grasslands of East Africa are called the savanna. Because the grazing animals here feed on different parts of the grass plant, there is usually enough to go around except in the dry season, when animals must constantly move to find food and water.

Use your Guide to Grass-Eaters to match the part of grass with the animal that eats it. Lay the guide over the Tropical Grass-land Grass-Eaters diagram. Lift each numbered flap and fold it over the plant. When you know which animal eats which part of the plant, write its name in the Animal column of the Food for All table.

Food for All		
Flap Number	**Grass Part**	**Animal**
1	top	
2	middle	
3	bottom	

Activity: NIBBLERS

Purpose   To determine why grass can survive being nibbled by animals.

Materials   potting soil
7-ounce (210-ml) paper cup

> trowel
> clump of grass
> pencil
> saucer
> tap water
> ruler
> marking pen

Procedure

1. Put the soil in the cup.

2. With permission, use the trowel to dig up a clump of grass that will fit in the paper cup. Choose a clump that has at least three stems, and make sure you dig up as many of the grass roots as possible.

3. Plant the grass in the soil.

4. Use the pencil to punch three or four holes on the side of the cup around the bottom edge.

5. Set the cup in a saucer.

6. Moisten the soil with water and keep the soil moist, but not wet, during the experiment.

7. Use the diagram to locate the **nodes** (where leaves grow from a stem) on each grass stem.

8. Use the ruler and pen to mark three equal sections on one of the stems between two nodes at the top of the stem.

9. Repeat step 8 for the other two stems, marking the second and third highest pair of nodes, respectively.

10. Set the plant in an area where it will receive sunlight all or most of the day.

11. At the end of 7 days, measure the distance between the marks on the stems.

Results   The distance between the lower node and the first mark above this node increases the most on all the stems. Any

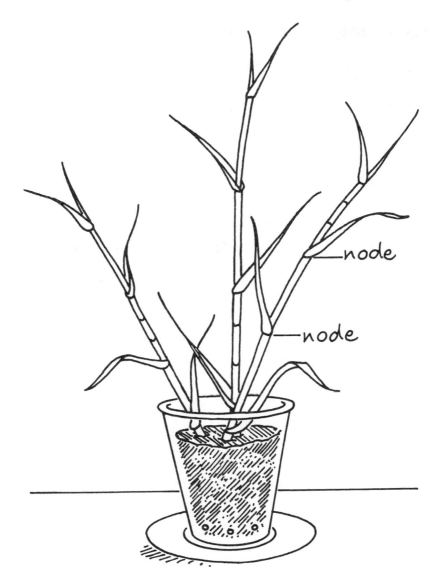

increase in distance between the remaining marks is slight to none as the marks approach the higher node.

Why?   Grasses grow above each node along the stem, not from the tips as other plants do. Even with the loss of large portions of stem, lower areas continue to grow. This type of growth allows grass to survive nibbling by animals.

Solution to Exercise

Think!

- Under flap 1 is a zebra.

  Zebras eat the top of grass stems.

Think!

- Under flap 2 is a wildebeest.

  Wildebeests eat the middle part of grass stems.

Think!

- Under flap 3 is a Thomson's gazelle.

  Thomson's gazelles eat the bottom part of grass stems.

14
Hot Spot

Learning about Plants and Animals in Desert Biomes

What You Need to Know

A desert is most often thought of as being very hot, dry, and lifeless. While deserts are the driest places on earth, not all of them are hot. Some deserts, such as the Gobi Desert in Mongolia and the Great Basin Desert in North America, are covered with snow during part of the year. Deserts are grouped into two types by temperature: **cold desert** (a desert with daytime temperatures below freezing for part of the year) and **hot desert** (a desert with hot daytime temperatures for most of the year).

Deserts lose more water through evaporation than they gain from precipitation. An area is considered a desert if it receives less than 10 inches (25 cm) of precipitation a year. Most have less than 4 inches (10 cm) of precipitation a year. The polar ice caps are examples of cold deserts that often receive less than 2 inches (5 cm) of precipitation per year.

Not only is there a shortage of precipitation in a desert, but the precipitation doesn't fall evenly throughout the year. In some deserts it may not rain the whole year, and then a violent thunderstorm may dump 5 inches (12.5 cm) or more of rain at once. Most of this water runs off or evaporates before plants and animals have a chance to use it. Areas that may receive more than

10 inches (25 cm) of rain per year, but where the evaporation rate during the year is greater than the yearly amount of rainfall, are also considered deserts. Evaporation rate is increased by high temperatures and strong winds.

The thought that all deserts are lifeless wastelands is far from true. Some desert areas have more varieties of plants and animals than wetter areas. These organisms have special adaptations that allow them to store water or obtain it from their food. Many plants are **ephemerals** (organisms that have a short life cycle). Ephemerals can grow and produce seeds during a short rainy season or, in cold deserts, during the short summer when the ice and snow melt. In hot deserts, the leaves and stems of many desert plants have a thick waxlike coating that prevents water loss.

All plants lose water through tiny pores on the surface of their leaves called **stomata**. The stomata are able to open and close to take in and release water vapor. Many desert plants have fewer stomata, and some only open their stomata when less water evaporates, which is after the sun sets and the temperature drops. Some desert plants have few leaves or no leaves at all. The leaves on desert plants may roll or turn in a direction away from the sun during the heat of the day to reduce the amount of leaf surface exposed to the sun.

Desert animals get water in various ways. Small animals can get water from the food they eat. The pack rat, for example, eats **succulent plants** (plants that have thick, fleshy leaves or stems for storing water), such as cacti. Larger animals get some of their water from food, but many must wander constantly in search of a water hole from which to drink. Some animals **estivate** (spend the summer in a sleeplike condition of partial or total inactivity) until it rains. Estivation should not be confused with hibernation, which is a similar sleeplike condition of some animals that occurs during winter.

Many animals in hot deserts stay cool by keeping out of the sun during the day and looking for food at night. They find cooler,

shady places under rocks, trees, and shrubs, and some dig tunnels under the soil. Some adaptations also keep animals cooler, such as the oversize ears of jackrabbits and foxes. In these animals, air flowing over the ears cools the blood in the blood vessels near the surface of the skin of the ears. This cooled blood is then carried to the rest of the body.

Exercises

1. Use the bar graph to determine the following:

   a. How many regions are considered a desert?

   b. Which is the driest region?

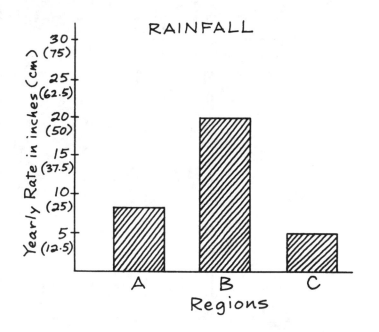

2. Use the bar graph on the next page to determine which area is considered a desert.

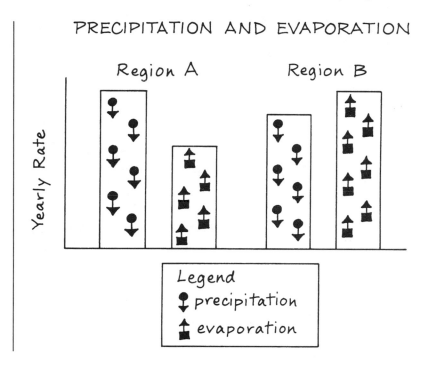

PRECIPITATION AND EVAPORATION

Region A   Region B

Yearly Rate

Legend
precipitation
evaporation

Activity: EXPANDABLE SKIN

Purpose To demonstrate how some cactus plants store water.

Materials typing paper
1-gallon (4-liter) plastic food bag (such as a produce bag)
tape

Procedure

1. Fold the paper like a fan, beginning at one short end. Each fold should be about ½ inch (1.3 cm) wide.

2. Fold the plastic bag in thirds.

3. Lay the folded bag on top of the folded paper with the bottom of the bag even with the edge of the paper. Tape the bottom of the bag to the edge of the paper.

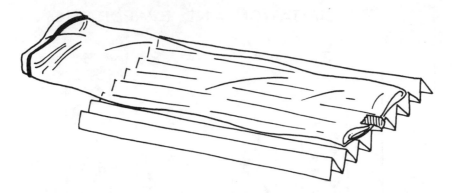

4. Wrap the paper so that it forms a cylinder around the bag. Secure the ends of the paper with tape.

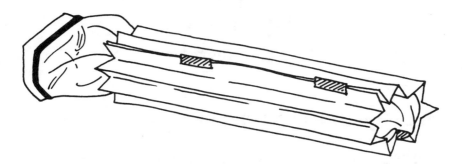

5. Stand the paper cylinder on a table with the open end of the plastic bag up.

6. Observe the size of the paper cylinder.

7. Open the top of the bag. Blow into the bag while holding it with your hand.

8. Keep the air inside the bag by squeezing the top closed with your hand.

9. Again, observe the size of the paper cylinder.

10. Release the bag, then use your hands to gently squeeze the paper pleats back into place.

11. Again observe the size of the cylinder.

Results The cylinder enlarges when the bag inside is filled with air. Squeezing the cylinder returns it to its smaller folded shape.

Why? Adding air to the bag causes it to enlarge. As the bag enlarges, it pushes outward on the paper cylinder. This outward pressure causes the pleats in the paper to unfold and the cylinder to increase in size. As the pleats unfold, the shape of the cylinder changes as the surface becomes smoother.

This experiment demonstrates the way some cacti, such as the saguaro, hold extra water. Saguaros grow very high and have trunks that are pleated like the paper. A 20-foot (6-m) plant may store more than 100 gallons (380 liters) of water. This water pushes outward, causing the saguaro's pleated surface to unfold. Cacti may increase in size as much as 20 percent during the rainy season. During times without rain, cacti use their stored water and shrink back to a smaller size and shape. Cacti can remain alive through long droughts because of their ability to store water.

Solutions to Exercises

1a. *Think!*

- A desert is a region that receives less than 10 inches (25 cm) of rainfall in a year.

- How many bars are shorter than the 10-inch (25-cm) mark?

    There are two desert regions, A and C.

b. *Think!*

- Which is the shortest bar?

    Region C is the driest.

2. *Think!*

- When the yearly evaporation rate is greater than the yearly precipitation, an area is considered a desert.

- Which region's bar for evaporation rate is higher than its bar for precipitation rate?

    Region B is a desert.

15
Highlands

Learning about Plants and Animals in Mountain Biomes

What You Need to Know

The higher you go up a mountain, the colder the climate becomes. This is because the amount of materials in the atmosphere that reflect and absorb energy from the sun, such as dust and water vapor, decreases with height. This results in a general decrease in temperature.

The type of plant growth changes from the bottom to the top of the mountain because of climate changes. This means that mountains have different climate zones, each with its own typical plants and animals. It is possible to have many ecosystems on the same mountain, from desert on the lower slopes to forest, grassland, tundra, and bare rock and snow as you progress to the top.

Many mountains have a tree line and a snow line. The **tree line** is the height above which the climate is too cold for trees to grow. The **snow line** is the height above which snow stays year-round. The **elevation** (height above sea level) of the tree and snow lines of a mountain depends on how close the mountain is to the equator. Both are higher the closer the mountain is to the equator, because the overall climate is warmer near the equator.

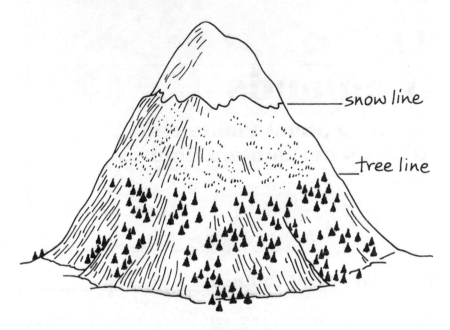

Mountain wildlife is also different on the lower slopes from that at the peak. The animals of the desert, forest, grassland, and tundra of a mountain have similar characteristics to the animals in the same type of biomes in lower elevations of the earth.

But some mountain animals also have special adaptive characteristics. One example is the takin, which has strong legs and large hooves to climb steep slopes. Animals with **cloven hooves** (split hooves), such as mountain goats and sheep, are better able to keep their balance on a mountainside, because their cloven hooves move independently and adjust to the uneven surface of the mountainside.

On high slopes, some wildlife must cope with cold temperatures. Thick fur coats and layers of fat are two ways in which animals that live high in the mountains stay warm. In addition to being cold, the air at higher elevations contains less oxygen. Many animals that breathe this thin air have larger than average hearts and lungs. These larger organs help them to get the needed amount of oxygen from the thin air.

Studying the plants and wildlife of a mountain can be as varied as studying the plants and wildlife across the earth from the equator to the poles.

Exercises

1. Study the figures of the mountain zones to identify the following:

   a. The mountain farthest from the equator.

   b. Mount Kenya, the mountain closest to the equator.

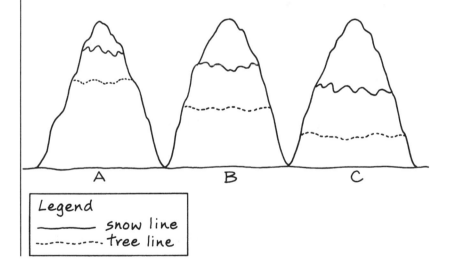

2. Study the bar graphs to determine which mountain correctly shows the relationship of the oxygen content of air to elevation.

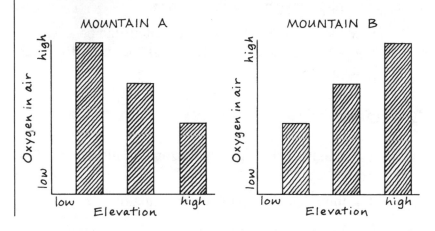

Activity: SHOCK ABSORBERS

Purpose To determine why mountain goats are able to move around surefootedly on rocky slopes.

Materials child's sock
1 cup (250 ml) uncooked rice
9-ounce (270-ml) plastic drinking cup with a flat bottom
white paper
marking pen

Procedure

1. Fill the sock with enough rice that the sock fits inside the cup.

2. Tie a knot in the top of the sock.

3. Place the sock in the cup.

4. Set the cup in the center of the paper on a level surface, such as a tabletop. With the pen, trace the outline of the bottom of the cup on the paper.

5. Raise the cup about 6 inches (15 cm) above the circle drawn on the paper. Make an effort to position the cup above the paper so that it will fall straight down and land in the circle when dropped.

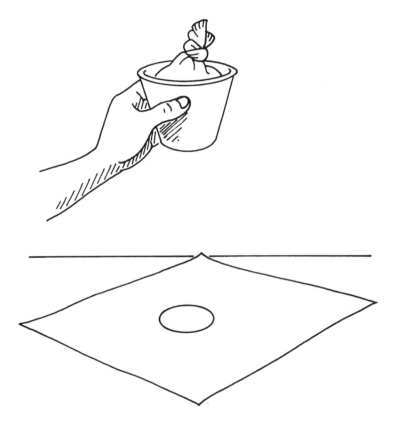

6. Drop the cup.

7. Observe where the cup lands, and note any movement it makes after landing.

8. Repeat steps 5 to 7 four times.

9. Remove the sock from the cup.

10. Hold the sock about 6 inches (15 cm) above the circle. Make an effort to position the sock so that it will fall straight down and land in the circle when dropped.

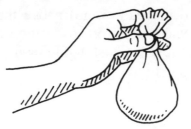

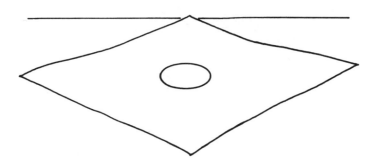

11. Drop the sock.

12. Observe where the sock lands, and note any movement it makes after landing.

13. Repeat steps 10 to 12 four times.

Results When the sock is in the cup, it lands in the circle, but the cup usually bounces upon landing and either falls over or moves partly out of the circle. The sock alone lands in the circle each time and does not bounce.

Why? Newton's third law of motion states that for every action there is an equal but opposite reaction. This means that the paper and tabletop push up on the cup and sock with the same force that the cup and sock push down on the paper and tabletop. This upward push causes the cup to bounce. The tabletop and paper also push up on the sock alone, but the sock does not bounce because, unlike the cup, its surface is soft and flexible.

Flexibility allows parts of the sock to move up and down without moving the entire sock. This independent movement allows the sock to absorb the shock of landing and not bounce around. The soft pads in the center of the hard hooves of a goat, like the sock, also act as shock absorbers. When a goat walks or leaps from one rock to the next, any bounce is absorbed by the soft, flexible footpads.

Solutions to Exercises

1a. *Think!*

- The mountain farthest from the equator has the lowest tree and snow lines.

  Mountain C is farthest from the equator.

b. *Think!*

- The mountain closest to the equator has the highest tree and snow lines.

  Mountain A is closest to the equator.

2. *Think!*

- The oxygen content of air decreases with elevation.
- Which bar graph shows the shortest bar (oxygen content) on the right side of the graph (highest elevation)?

  Mountain A correctly shows the relationship of the oxygen content of air to elevation.

16
Watery Home

Learning about Plants and Animals in Ocean Ecosystems

What You Need to Know

About three-fourths of the earth is covered by water. The largest bodies of water are called **oceans.** The oceans are not actually separate bodies of water, but one great ocean, making the ocean the largest ecosystem on earth.

Plants and animals of the ocean are called **marine life**. These can be divided into three groups, depending on the depth at which they are found:

1. **Benthos:** This group includes animals, such as clams, and plants, such as kelp, that live in or on the bottom of the ocean regardless of water depth. Most plants live in shallow water.

2. **Nekton:** These are animals, such as fish and whales, that move independently of water currents between the bottom and surface of the ocean.

3. **Plankton:** These small to microscopic organisms live near the ocean's surface and are carried along by the currents. Animal plankton are called **zooplankton**, and plant plankton are called **phytoplankton**.

The depth of the ocean varies, with the greatest depth being about 36,000 feet (10.9 km) in the Mariana Trench in the Pacific Ocean south of Guam. About 90 percent of all marine life exists in the upper 488 feet (150 m) of the ocean, where the waters are warm and penetrated by the sun's light. This zone of the ocean is called the **sunlight zone**. There are different types of animals at different depths of this zone. Some move up and down in the zone. For example, some fish remain far below the surface during bright daytime and come up at night to feed.

A deeper, colder, more dimly lit area called the **twilight zone** extends from the bottom of the sunlight zone down to about 3,000 feet (900 m). Plants cannot grow in this shadowy layer. Animals in this area are less numerous than those living in the warm, sunny layer above them. Some of the fish in this zone

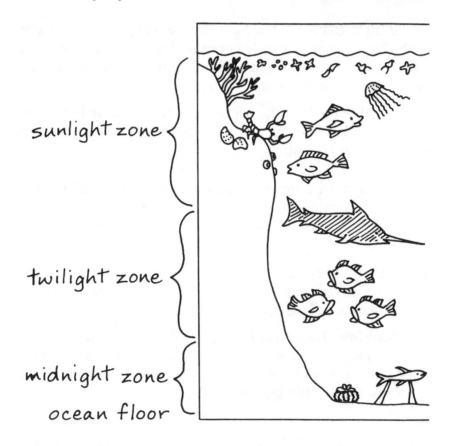

swim up to the sunlight zone at night to feed, but others prey on fish in their own area and/or eat falling dead matter that drifts down from the sunlight zone.

The bottom ocean zone, called the **midnight zone,** is cold and without light. It extends from about 3,000 feet (900 m) down to the ocean floor. Only about 1 percent of marine life can survive below 3,000 feet (900 m), and they mainly feed off of the falling dead bodies of organisms that live in the upper levels.

The habitats for marine life range from the water's edge at the shoreline to the depths of the ocean and from one shoreline to the next. As on land, life in the ocean is not equally distributed. Most of the open waters are deserted. The most populated areas are along coastlines and in the waters of the Arctic and Antarctic.

Exercise

Using only the letters you find in the fish drawing, see how many ocean words you can come up with. Here are a few hints to get you started:

- Each blank stands for one letter on the fish's scales.
- The letters given for each word provide clues to the missing letters (each letter can be used more than once!).
- Fill in the missing letters to discover the ocean words, which have all been used in this chapter.

1. w _ _ _ r

2. f _ _ h

3. p _ a _ k _ _ _

4. b _ n _ _ o _

5. ma _ _ _ e

6. _ el _

7. _ _ k _ o _

8. w _ a _ _

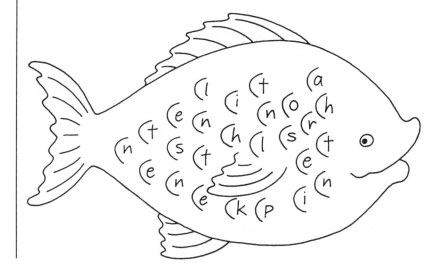

Activity: UNDERWATER FOREST

Purpose   To build a model of kelp.

Materials   scissors
empty 2-quart (2-liter) plastic soda bottle
ruler
aluminum foil
pipe cleaner
2 round plastic fishing corks, 1 inch (2.5 cm) in
   diameter, with spring-type clips
rock
tap water
adult helper

Procedure

1. Ask an adult to cut the top off the soda bottle to make an open container about 8 inches (20 cm) tall.

2. Cut an 8-by-6-inch (20-by-15-cm) strip of foil.

3. Fold the foil strip in half lengthwise four times.

4. Wrap about 2 inches (5 cm) of one end of the foil strip around the center of the pipe cleaner.

5. Clip the bottom of one cork to the foil strip 2 inches (5 cm) above the pipe cleaner.

6. Clip the bottom of the second cork 2 inches (5 cm) above the first cork.

7. Cut two long triangles from the aluminum foil, each with a base of 1 inch (2.5 cm) and sides of 6 inches (15 cm).

8. Clip the top of each cork to the base of one of the foil triangles.

9. Wrap the pipe cleaner around the rock.

10. Fill about three-quarters of the soda bottle with water.

11. Carefully lower the rock and attachments into the water.

Results   The corks float at different depths along with the attached foil triangles.

Why?   Underwater forests of tall, brown **algae** (simple plant-like organisms found in water or on wet surfaces), called **kelp**, grow in cool coastal waters. These thick strands of kelp provide living spaces for hundreds of different kinds of ocean organisms. Kelp varies in height from 1.5 feet (4.5 m) to 198 feet (60 m).

Most kelps consist of at least four distinguishable parts: the holdfast (represented by pipe cleaner), the stipe (foil strip), the float (cork), and the blade (foil triangle). The holdfast is a root-like structure that clings to rocks and other hard surfaces on the ocean floor, keeping the kelp from floating to the surface. The stipe is a stemlike structure to which the blades are attached.

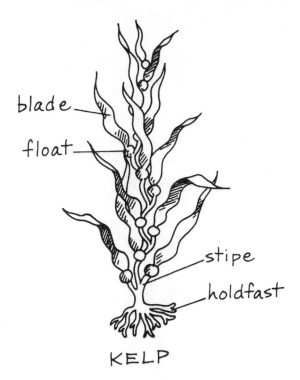

blade

float

stipe

holdfast

KELP

The float is an air-filled structure at the base of each blade that lifts the kelp so that it stands upright. The blade is a leaflike structure where photosynthesis occurs.

Solution to Exercise

Think!

The words are:

1. water
2. fish
3. plankton
4. benthos

5. marine
6. kelp
7. nekton
8. whale

17
Water Problems
The Problems of Water Pollution and How to Solve Them

What You Need to Know

Water is one of the earth's most valuable resources. An adequate supply of clean water is needed for your survival as well as the survival of plants and animals. People often use more water than they really need. Each day the average American uses about 125 gallons (500 liters) of water for drinking, cooking, cleaning, and flushing. Another 1,800 gallons (7,200 liters) per person is used by farmers to grow the crops you eat and by industry to produce the products you use.

When you flush, bathe, brush your teeth, wash clothes, or rinse something down the drain, the water goes to sewage treatment plants to be cleaned. Here **pollutants** (substances that destroy the purity of water, land, and air), such as food waste and dirt, are removed. The water is then treated to kill harmful bacteria before it is released into waterways. However, not all pollutants are removed from this water.

City streets are washed clean of oil, grime, chemicals, and litter by the rain. This dirty water usually flows into underground drains and eventually is released, untreated, into waterways. Rain also washes chemical fertilizers added to the soil into waterways. In some countries, laws control the type of materials that factories can dump into waterways. However, even with regulations, some wastes from factories still get dumped, either accidentally or intentionally, into waterways. Pollutants that find their way into waterways endanger the plants and animals living in and near the water.

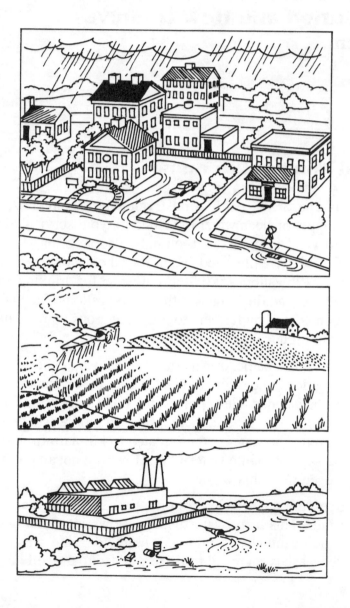

Some chemical wastes dumped into bodies of water actually provide nutrients that promote excessive growth for algae. As the algae die, the decomposing organisms remove oxygen from the water, causing the death of other organisms, such as fish.

What can you do? One individual might only make a small change, but there are many millions of people living on the earth. Multiply a small change by several million and large changes will occur. Start making a difference today by conserving water. Remember, the less water you run down the drain, the fewer chemicals you add to the earth's waterways. These tips will help you and your family to conserve water:

- Reduce the water used when you flush. With an adult's help, place a brick or bottle filled with rocks in your toilet tank. These objects take up space and reduce the amount of water needed to fill the tank.

   NOTE: Take care not to damage the flushing mechanism in the tank.

- Take short showers instead of bathing in a tub. The amount of water usually needed for a shower is about one-half that needed to fill a bathtub.
- Don't allow the water to run while you brush your teeth.
- Turn faucets off so that they do not drip.
- Run the dishwasher only when you have a full load.
- Run the washing machine only when you have a full load.

Exercises

1. If ½ gallon (2 liters) of water is lost from a dripping faucet each hour, how much water is wasted in a week?

2. Each time a toilet is flushed, an average of 5 gallons (20 liters) of water is used. If you average 8 flushes per day, how many gallons of water do you use in a week?

Activity: POLLUTION DILUTION

Purpose To show how adding substances to water affects pollution.

Materials cup
quart (liter) jar
gallon (4-liter) jug, with lid
tap water
red food coloring
spoon
adult helper

Procedure

1. Fill the cup, jar, and jug three-fourths full with water.

2. Add and stir in 2 drops of food coloring to the water in the cup.

3. Pour all but a small amount of the water from the cup into the jar and stir.

4. Pour all but a small amount of the water from the jar into the jug.

5. Ask an adult to place the lid on the jug and shake the jug back and forth to mix thoroughly.

6. Compare the color of the water left in the cup and jar with the color of the water in the jug.

Results The water is dark red in the cup, pale red in the jar, and pale pink to colorless in the jug.

Why? The red color is most intense in the cup because the **molecules** (the smallest parts of a substance that have all the characteristics of the substance) of red coloring are close together and reflect more red light to your eyes. When this colored water is added to clean water, the color molecules spread evenly throughout the water. By the time the color molecules are added to the clean water in the jug, they are far enough apart to become very pale to invisible because of their small size.

This is what happens with some water pollutants. The material may be visible where it is initially dumped into a river, but as it flows downstream and becomes mixed with more water, it can no longer be seen with the naked eye. This does not mean that the pollutant is gone. Animal and plant life in a stream is affected by pollutants many miles from the source. The degree of harm to the animal depends on the type of pollutant and how much water has been added in order to **dilute** (lessen the strength by mixing with another material, usually water) the pollutant.

Solutions to Exercises

1. *Think!*

   • There are 24 hours in a day. The amount of water wasted each day is

24 × ½ gallon (2 liters) = 12 gallons (48 liters)

- There are 7 days in a week. The amount of water wasted in a week is

7 × 12 gallons (48 liters) = ?

The dripping faucet wastes 84 gallons (336 liters) in a week.

2. *Think!*

- The amount of water used each day is

8 × 5 gallons (20 liters) = 40 gallons (160 liters)

- One week has 7 days. The amount of water needed for flushing in 7 days is

7 × 40 gallons (160 liters) = ?

In a week, 280 gallons (1,120 liters) of water are used for flushing.

18
Global Warming
What the Greenhouse Effect Is

What You Need to Know

The amount of **solar energy** (energy from the sun) that reaches the earth is called **insolation**. The input diagram here shows that out of 340 units of energy directed toward the earth, only 238 units are absorbed by atmospheric gases, clouds, and the

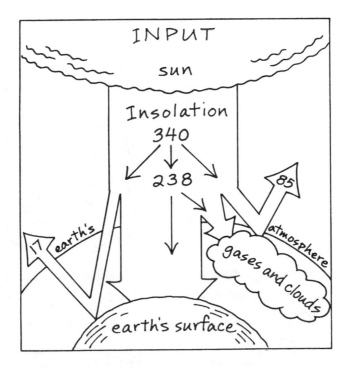

earth's surface. The remaining 102 units are reflected back into space.

The temperature of the earth is kept warm due to the atmosphere and gases in the atmosphere called **greenhouse gases** (mainly carbon dioxide and water vapor). These gases trap warmth from the sun and keep some of the insolation from being reflected back into space. Solar energy enters the glass and warms the inside of a **greenhouse** (a structure, usually made of glass or clear plastic, that provides a protected, controlled environment for raising plants indoors). For this reason, the warming of the earth is called the **greenhouse effect**.

The output diagram shows 453 units of energy moving away from the earth. Of these, 300 energy units are reflected back to the earth by clouds and greenhouse gases. The remaining 153 units, combined with 85 units that move away from clouds, to-

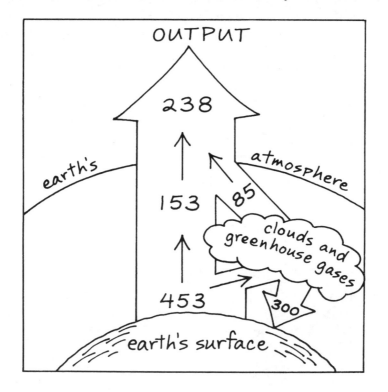

tal 238 energy units that escape into space. This means that the amount of input energy is equal to the total amount of output energy. As long as the input and output energy remain equal, the average surface temperature of the earth will remain the same.

The average surface temperature of the earth depends on the amount of greenhouse gases in the atmosphere. An increase in the gases would result in an increase in the average temperature, and a decrease in the gases would cause a decrease in temperature.

Carbon dioxide, one of the greenhouse gases, is responsible for much of the warming of the earth. Carbon dioxide is a product of respiration, but a large amount is produced by burning fossil fuels. A **fossil fuel** is any deposit of fossil materials, such as petroleum, natural gas, or coal, that can be burned to produce energy. **Fossils** are the traces of the remains of prehistoric animals and plants. As the population of the earth increases, more fossil fuels are being burned, so the amount of carbon dioxide being produced is increasing. Many scientists predict a rise in the average temperature of the earth if the amount of fossil fuels burned is not changed.

Trees can help reduce the amount of carbon dioxide in the air. They use carbon dioxide in the photosynthesis reaction to make food. **Deforestation** (the stripping away of trees), as well as the burning of fossil fuels, contributes to an increase in carbon dioxide in the atmosphere. Recycling paper products and planting seedling trees where mature trees have been removed can help prevent deforestation.

It is difficult to make accurate predictions about the effect of a warming of the earth's average temperature, but here are some possibilities. A major change in weather patterns, such as more droughts or tropical storms, could make warm areas become unbearably hot. Another problem might be that warming would cause polar ice caps and the glaciers to melt, enlarging the oceans and causing flooding of seashore areas. This would affect the entire food web along coastlines.

You can help to reduce the threat of global warming by recycling paper products, decreasing the use of fossil fuels, and using alternative energy sources that do not produce carbon dioxide. Remember that one way electricity is produced is through the burning of fossil fuels. So reducing the use of electricity reduces the use of fossil fuels. Consider this list of possible ways to reduce the use of fossil fuels and think of others:

- Ride a school bus or carpool to school instead of being driven in the family car.
- Turn down the heat and wear warmer clothes in the winter.
- Don't leave the refrigerator door open while you decide what to eat or drink.
- Turn off lights, stereos, TVs, and the like as soon as you are finished with them.
- Don't use air-conditioning more than necessary.

Exercises

Study the diagram and answer the following questions. Note that the solar energy coming in is broken into ten equal parts. Each part represents 10 percent (10%) of the total energy.

1. What percentage of solar energy is reflected by gases and clouds in the earth's atmosphere?
2. What percentage of solar energy is reflected by the earth's surface?
3. How much solar energy is not reflected back into space?

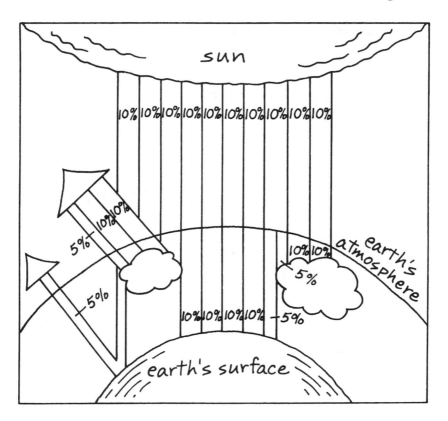

Activity: BOUNCE BACK

Purpose   To simulate the greenhouse effect.

Materials   2 cups (500 ml) soil
1 lidded jar (tall enough to hold one of the thermometers)
2 thermometers

Procedure

1. Put the soil in the jar.

2. Place one of the thermometers inside the jar and secure the lid.

3. Place the jar near a window in direct sunlight, and place the second thermometer next to the jar.

4. Observe the temperature readings on both thermometers after 30 minutes.

Results The temperature reading inside the closed jar is higher than that outside the jar.

Why? The jar is a small model of a greenhouse. A greenhouse is made of glass or clear plastic, which allows solar energy to pass through and heat the contents.

Like a greenhouse, solar energy enters and warms the earth's atmosphere. A greenhouse warms mainly because it is closed and the cooler air outside is prevented from mixing with the warm air inside. The earth warms because solar energy strikes the earth's surface and the surface gives off heat. Most of this heat is absorbed by the greenhouse gases, trapping the heat close to the earth. For more information about the greenhouse effect, see "Hot Box" on pages 24–27 in *Janice VanCleave's Weather* (New York: Wiley, 1995).

Solutions to Exercises

1. *Think!*

- Three parts of solar energy reflect off a cloud.
- The sum of the percentages of all three parts equals the total amount of energy reflected.

  10% + 10% + 5% = ?

  The percentage of solar energy reflected by the earth's atmosphere is 25 percent.

2. *Think!*

- One 5% part of solar energy reflects off the earth's surface.

  The percentage of solar energy reflected by the earth's surface is 5 percent.

3. *Think!*

- The cloud receives three parts of solar energy.
- The sum of the percentages of all three parts equals the total energy absorbed by the cloud.

  10% + 10% + 5% = 25%

- The earth's surface receives five parts of solar energy.

- The sum of the percentages of all five parts equals the total energy absorbed by the earth's surface.

  10% + 10% + 10% + 10% + 5% = 45%

- The amount absorbed by the cloud plus the amount absorbed by the earth's surface equals the total energy absorbed.

  25% + 45% = ?

The percentage of solar energy absorbed, or not reflected back into space, is 70 percent.

19
Good and Bad

How Plastics Affect the Environment

What You Need to Know

Plastics are very useful and usually inexpensive materials. They can be water-resistant, lightweight, and not easily broken. Since plastic foam acts as an insulator, it is used to hold and maintain the temperature of food. Plastic foam is also so light that it floats and therefore can be used to make life preservers.

But for all the benefits plastics have, they can also be bad for the environment. Most plastics last a long time. While it is good to have long-lasting products, it can also be bad because plastics are difficult to get rid of. To dispose of plastic, it is either buried in a solid waste disposal area called a **sanitary landfill**, burned, or recycled. Burning produces toxic air pollutants. Burying may remove the plastic from sight, but most plastics are not **biodegradable** (capable of being broken down into nonharmful substances by the action of living organisms, especially bacteria). This means that plastics in landfills will be there, unchanged, for hundreds of years. Waste plastics can also end up in our waters, and small pieces of floating plastic can be mistaken for food by fish, turtles, and other water-dwelling organisms. Plastic can kill these organisms.

Scientists are finding ways to make plastics that are less harmful to the environment. The addition of cellulose to plastics

makes them decompose more easily. But it is still not determined how well these plastics will decompose or whether they will find their way into water systems and cause water pollution.

Some, but not all, plastics are being recycled. The plastics are cleaned, cut into pieces, melted, and re-formed into many different products, such as skis, surf boards, pipes, park benches, and fiberfill stuffing. Since not all plastics are recycled at this time, this is not the total solution to the plastic disposal problem. However, it is a better solution than burning or burying it.

Exercises

1. For each figure, identify whether the use of plastic is good or bad.

A

plastic foam

B

plastic foam

C

plastic foam

COCOA

D

plastic

Landfill

plastic

2. It is difficult to completely avoid the use of plastic. Determine which of the following actions would allow you to
   help with the plastic problem.

   a. Reuse plastic containers.

   b. Burn discarded plastics.

   c. Buy products made of natural materials such as paper
      or wood instead of plastic.

   d. Take a cloth bag to the grocery store instead of using
      plastic bags.

Activity: FOAMY

Purpose   To make simulated plastic foam.

Materials   1 cup (250 ml) cold tap water
                2-quart (2-liter) bowl
                2 tablespoons (30 ml) dishwashing liquid
                whisk
                mixing spoon
                1-cup (250-ml) measuring cup
                timer
                1-tablespoon (15-ml) measuring spoon

Procedure

1. Pour the water into the bowl.

2. Add the dishwashing liquid to the water in the bowl.

3. Use the whisk to beat the liquid until you have made a big
   mound of foam.

4. Use the mixing spoon to fill the measuring cup with foam.

   NOTE: Be careful not to transfer any liquid to the cup.

5. Put the cup where it will not be disturbed.

6. Observe the foam as often as possible for 4 hours.

7. After 4 hours, or when all the foam has changed to a liquid, use the measuring spoon to measure the liquid in the cup.

Results   When foamy, the bubbles fill the cup. After the bubbles have popped, the cupful of foam changes to about 2 tablespoons (30 ml) of liquid.

Why?   Beating the liquid produces bubbles filled with air. The foam is mostly air. When the cup is allowed to sit, the bubbles break, the air escapes, and the foam turns back to a soapy liquid. Like the soap foam, plastic foam is full of air. But unlike the soap foam, the bubbles don't break unless pressure is applied, so plastic foam stays the same size. Because plastic foam is mostly air, large materials made with this plastic are very lightweight and easy to transport. Air does not transmit energy easily, so air-filled plastic is a good insulator, which is good. However, such plastics take up large amounts of space in garbage dumps, which is bad.

Solutions to Exercises

1a. *Think!*

- A life vest made of plastic foam would float. This could save the child's life if he or she fell into the water.

   In figure A, the use of plastic as a life vest is good.

b. *Think!*

- The fish thinks the piece broken from the plastic foam life buoy is food. The fish could die if it ate plastic.

   In figure B, plastic as food for fish is bad.

c. *Think!*

- The plastic foam used to make the cup is an insulator. This allows the liquid in the cup to stay warm longer.

   In figure C, the use of plastic as an insulating material for a cup is good.

d. *Think!*

- Most plastics are not biodegradable. Buried plastics will remain in landfills for hundreds of years.

   In figure D, plastic as landfill material is bad.

2a. *Think!*

- Reuse of plastic reduces the disposal problem.

b. *Think!*

- Burning plastic can produce toxic air pollutants.

c. *Think!*

- Natural materials, such as paper and wood, are much more biodegradable than plastic.

d. *Think!*

- The cloth bag can be used again and again and is bio-degradable when finally discarded as trash.

  Actions a, c, and d would allow you to help with the plastic problem.

20
Acid Rain

The Causes and Effects of Acid Rain

What You Need to Know

Acid rain is any kind of precipitation that contains larger than normal amounts of acid. Every **solution** (a mixture made by dissolving a substance in a liquid, such as water) is either acidic, basic, or neutral. The unit of measure for determining whether a solution is acidic, a basic, or neutral is called **pH**, and the scale used to measure pH is called the **pH scale**. The values on the pH scale range from 0 to 14. An **acid** solution, such as vinegar or normal rainwater, has a pH less than 7. Solutions with pH values greater than 7, such as milk of magnesia and eggs, are **bases** (the opposite of acid and capable of reducing

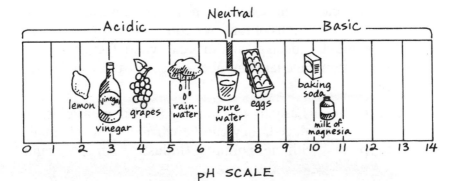

pH SCALE

the amount of acid in a substance). A pH of 0 is the highest acid value, and a pH of 14 is the highest base value. A pH of 7 indicates that a solution is **neutral** (neither acidic nor basic). Pure water is neutral.

Each whole-number difference between pH values indicates ten times the acid or base strength of adjacent values. Thus, a pH 2 solution is ten times more acidic than a pH 3 solution. The difference between pH 2 and pH 4 is two whole numbers. Thus, a solution with pH 2 is 10×10, or 100, times more acidic than a pH 4 solution.

Water that evaporates from the earth is neither acidic nor basic. It is neutral (pH 7). When this water vapor condenses, the liquid water mixes with atmospheric gases, such as carbon dioxide. Water plus normal amounts of carbon dioxide produces a weak acid with a pH between 5 and 6. Thus, normal rainwater is slightly acidic. The acid in normal rain can dissolve rocks, but it may take hundreds or even thousands of years to do so.

The low pH—high levels of acid—in acid rain is caused by the presence of air pollutants, such as sulfur dioxide and nitrogen oxides. These gases produce acids when combined with water. This acid precipitation falls to the earth, and some eventually finds its way to waterways.

Some air pollutants, such as the gases and dust from volcanic eruptions, are produced naturally. Air pollutants resulting from human action are mostly the result of burning fossil fuels, such as coal and oil. These fuels are burned to produce energy for such things as cars, homes, and businesses. The burning of fossil fuels releases millions of tons of pollutants into the air every year. The amount is much greater in areas where factories, electric power stations, and large numbers of cars, trucks, and buses are found.

While air pollutants usually rise and then fall in areas close to where they are produced, they can be carried by winds many miles to places with no polluting industry. Air pollutants

dropped by winds are called **dirty fallout. Prevailing winds** blow from one direction and, like all winds, are named for the direction they come from. An easterly prevailing wind comes from the east and blows toward the west. This means that areas to the west of an industrial area with easterly prevailing winds and to the east in areas with westerly prevailing winds are more likely to receive more dirty fallout.

Some air pollutants fall to the ground quickly without combining with moisture. These are called **dry deposits**. Others can build up and later combine with rainwater to form strong acid solutions. Pollutants that remain in the air can stay there for a week or more. During this time, some mix with moisture in the air to form acids before eventually falling. These are called **wet deposits**. Before falling, these pollutants often combine with other chemicals in the air to form additional pollutants, such as ozone. See Chapter 21, "Protector," for more information about formation and the polluting effects of ozone.

Acid rain slowly eats away buildings, monuments, and other structures made of rock. But an effect that causes great concern is that acid rain makes some lakes acidic. Normally, a lake has a pH of about 6.5 and supports many types of plants, insects, and fish. Other animals and birds also depend on lakes for food. High acid levels kill young fish that are hatching from their eggs.

Acids also cause poisonous minerals, such as aluminum and mercury, to be separated from the surrounding ground as the acid rain flows over the ground. These pollutants are carried over ground into the lakes. Birds that eat fish from lakes containing poisonous minerals also suffer. The shells of their eggs are affected: they become more fragile and are easily broken. The young birds that do hatch can have deformed bones or die.

There is evidence from all over the world that acid rain is affecting trees and forests. Often, acid rain weakens trees so that they are either killed when they blow over or attacked by insects and fungi. One of the outward signs of tree damage caused by acid rain is fewer leaves.

Exercises

1. Which areas on the map would receive the most dirty fallout due to an easterly prevailing wind?

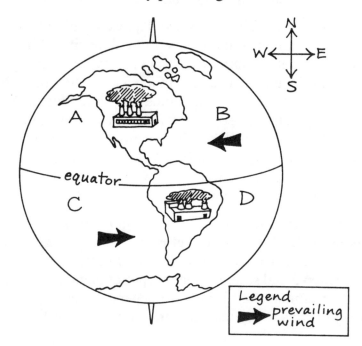

2. Determine how far an air pollutant is carried in 5 days by a wind moving 10 miles per hour (16 kph).

Activity: MISTY

Purpose   To demonstrate the effect of acid rain on plants.

Materials   2 quart (liter) spray bottles
distilled water
masking tape
marking pen
white vinegar
3 small house plants that are as similar as possible

Procedure

1. Fill one spray bottle with distilled water. Secure the lid.

2. Use the tape and pen to label the bottle "Water." This solution will be referred to as the water.

3. Fill the second spray bottle half full with distilled water, then add enough vinegar to fill the bottle.

4. Secure the lid and shake the bottle back and forth several times to mix its contents.

5. Label the second bottle "Acid." This solution will be referred to as the acid.

6. Label the plants "Water," "Acid," and "Dry." In the remaining steps, treat each plant exactly the same except for watering.

7. Spray the water on the soil of the plant labeled "Water" until it is damp but not wet. Count the number of squirts of water added to the plant.

8. Spray an equal amount of the acid on the soil of the plant labeled "Acid."

9. Do not water the plant labeled "Dry."

10. Place all 3 plants near a window so that they receive equal amounts of sunlight.

11. Once a day, spray the leaves of the plants labeled "Water" and "Acid" with three squirts of the appropriate solution.

12. Spray equal amounts of solution on the soil of the plants labeled "Water" and "Acid" as needed to keep the soil moist.

13. Do not water the plant labeled "Dry."

14. Observe the plants for 4 weeks or until one plant loses at least half its leaves or dies.

Results The dry plant dies. Its leaves become pale and eventually fall off. The leaves of the plant sprayed with acid become pale and some turn yellow before falling. This plant also dies. The amount of time for these results varies with the type of plant used. The plant sprayed with water remains healthy.

NOTE: These are the expected results, but an unhealthy plant could die even if sprayed with water.

Why?   Distilled water has a pH of 7. It is neutral—neither acidic nor basic. You can see that water is necessary for the survival of plants, because the dry plant dies without it. While plants remain healthy in slightly acidic rainfall, they cannot survive in low pH—high acid levels. The acid level of the vinegar solution is higher than most acid rain and higher than most common plants can endure, but some plants are more tolerant of acid and will survive for a longer period of time.

Solutions to Exercises

1. *Think!*

- Easterly prevailing winds come from the east and move toward the west.

  Areas A and C would receive the most dirty fallout due to prevailing winds.

2. *Think!*

- If there are 24 hours in 1 day, the number of hours in 5 days is

  $5 \times 24 = 120$ hours

- If the wind carries the pollutant 10 miles (16 km) in 1 hour, the distance the pollutant is carried in 120 hours is

  $10 \times 120 = ?$

  The wind carries the pollutant 1,200 miles (1,920 km) in 5 days.

21
Protector

What Ozone Is and How It Affects Living Things

What You Need to Know

The oxygen you breathe is made of two oxygen **atoms** (the tiny particles of which all things are made). The symbol for oxygen is O_2. Another form of oxygen, called **ozone**, is made up of three oxygen atoms, and its symbol is O_3.

One high-energy part of sunlight is called **ultraviolet (UV) light** and is responsible for the production of most ozone. In the upper atmosphere at a height of about 9 to 30 miles (15 to 50 km) above the earth's surface, UV rays cause oxygen to split apart into separate atoms. When the two atoms of oxygen combine with other oxygen molecules in the atmosphere, ozone molecules are produced.

Ozone collects in the upper atmosphere surrounding the earth, forming a layer called the **ozone layer**. The ozone layer is not a solid barrier, but scattered molecules of ozone gas. If all the ozone were compressed into a solid layer, it would be only about $\frac{1}{8}$ inch (0.3 cm) thick.

The ozone layer stops most of the sun's UV rays from reaching the earth. A few UV rays are necessary for life, but too many would actually cook you. You may have experienced being "cooked" by UV rays if you have ever stayed in the sun too long and got a sunburn. Ozone absorbs UV rays, but in the process the UV rays cause ozone to break down. Thus, there is a natural **ozone cycle** in which ozone breaks down and then re-forms.

If left alone, the ozone cycle would be balanced and the total amount of ozone in the ozone layer would remain unchanged. However, air pollutants called **CFCs** (chlorofluorocarbons) have caused the ozone layer to decrease in size. CFCs are gases that have been used in spray cans, air conditioners, and puffed-up plastic foam. When CFCs rise to the ozone layer, UV rays cause atoms of a gas called chlorine to break apart from the

CFCs. One free chlorine atom can cause thousands of ozone atoms to break apart, forming regular oxygen.

All the effects of a reduction in the ozone layer are not known, but it is certain that you could expect damage to your skin because of the increase in UV rays reaching the earth. Ozone is not entirely wonderful, however. Ozone is considered a pollutant in the lower atmosphere, where it is produced during lightning storms, by electrical equipment, and as a result of pollutants from automobiles. Breathing even low levels of ozone can lead to a sore throat, coughing, and other respiratory problems.

Exercises

1. Using the information provided for the oxygen atom as a guide, fill in the missing sections of the table.

Model	Symbol	Name
	O	oxygen atom
	O_2	

2. A hole in the ozone layer would allow high levels of UV light to pass through. This excess amount of UV rays may prevent plankton from making their own food, so they would die. Study the diagram and determine which of following describes a possible result of a hole in the ozone layer.

   a. Only the plankton die.

   b. Plankton and fish A die.

   c. Plankton, fish A, and fish B die.

plankton   fish A   fish B

Activity: SUNBLOCK

Purpose To simulate the effect of the ozone layer on light.

Materials clear plastic report folder
             sunblock lotion with high SPF rating
             sheet of newspaper
             masking tape
             modeling clay
             timer

Procedure

NOTE: The experiment works best if started at noon on a sunny day.

1. Use your fingers to coat one side of the folder with the lotion, making sure to apply it in an even layer. Wash your hands after applying the lotion.

2. Place the newspaper on a table outdoors.

3. Secure the paper by taping the corners to the table.

4. Use as many walnut-size balls of clay as needed to support the folder lotion side up over the center of the newspaper. Support the center of the folder with clay if necessary to keep it from touching the paper.

NOTE: You only want to test the effects of reduction of UV light, not the reduction of air. The folder is raised so that air can flow over the paper.

5. After 2 hours, remove the folder and compare the color of the newspaper under the area where the folder was placed with the color of the area outside the folder.

Results   The area of the newspaper covered by the folder remained white, while the area outside the plastic turned yellow.

Why?   The paper used to make newspaper has a yellow color before it is whitened by removing oxygen. Newspapers yellow with age, because over a period of time oxygen in the air gets added back into the paper. UV light from the sun speeds up the rate at which oxygen combines with the paper, thus reducing the time needed to yellow the paper. The sunblock lotion, like the ozone layer, prevented most of the UV light from hitting the paper.

Solutions to Exercises

1.

Model	Symbol	Name
	O	oxygen atom
	O_2	oxygen
	O_3	ozone

2. *Think!*

- Plankton are food for fish A, which is food for fish B.
- Without plankton, fish A dies.
- Without fish A, fish B dies.

The answer is C. Plankton, fish A, and fish B all will die if the plankton are killed.

22
Buildup

Where Most of Your Garbage Goes

What You Need to Know

What happens to the garbage your family creates? When the garbage truck picks up your garbage, does a wizard magically make it disappear? No! Your trash and the trash of millions of other people is either buried in a sanitary landfill, **incinerated** (burned to ashes), or recycled.

Open dumps contain waste that is allowed to remain exposed over long periods of time. Dumps are feeding grounds for insects, rats, and other disease-carrying animals. They smell, and they create a fire hazard. Dumps also allow **leachate** (a mixture of rainwater and other liquids that come from garbage) to seep into underground water.

Open dumps in the United States are being replaced with **sanitary landfills**. These differ from dumps in that they contain specially designed liners that protect the environment by keeping the waste and leachate sealed within the ground. Leachate drains to the bottom of the landfill, where it is pumped out. It is then treated either at the landfill or at a sewage treatment plant before being released into waterways.

Garbage is dumped into the landfill and compacted by bulldozers. When the landfill is full, it is covered with clay, then soil is

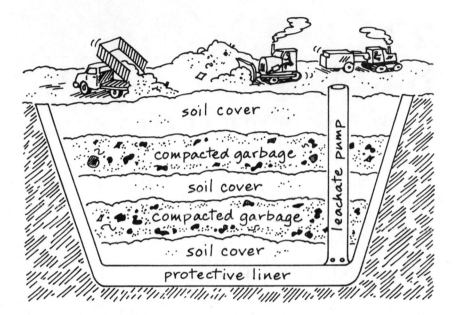

placed over the clay. Grass, plants, and trees are planted in the soil. These areas can be used for parks or other recreational areas.

There are about 6,000 landfills in the United States, and although they are better than open dumps, they are not the total answer to garbage disposal. They must be close to communities, and they require specific types of soil and geological conditions. Places that meet these requirements are becoming more difficult to find, and those being used are filling up much faster than expected. Landfills that are not correctly designed and managed do not protect the environment.

Exercises

1. Use the bar graph to complete the following statements about garbage disposal:

   a. Most garbage is ____.

   b. Only 13 percent of most garbage is ____.

GARBAGE DISPOSAL

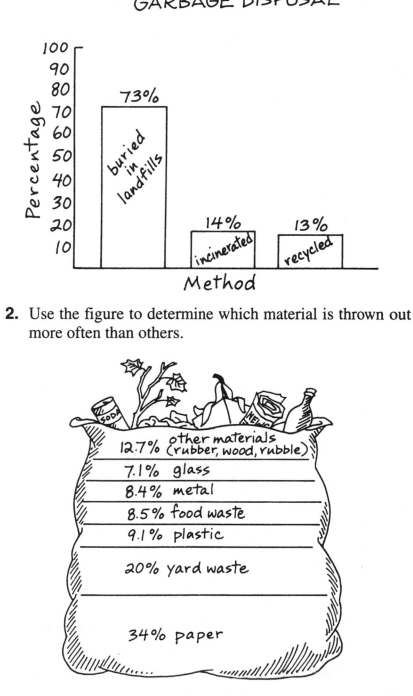

2. Use the figure to determine which material is thrown out more often than others.

Activity: FILL 'ER UP

Purpose To see how different materials change in a landfill.

Materials scissors
ruler
plastic trash bag
2 shoe boxes
masking tape
enough soil to fill both shoe boxes
large bowl
tap water
2 sets of test materials: newspaper, orange peel,
    aluminum foil, plastic lid
magnifying lens

Procedure

1. Cut two 22-by-22-inch (55-by-55-cm) pieces from the trash bag.

2. Line each shoe box with one piece of plastic.

3. Secure the plastic lining with tape.

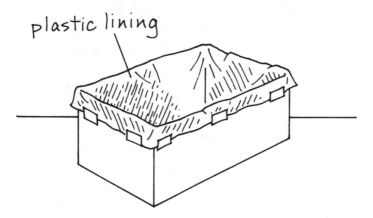

4. Place the soil in the bowl and add enough water to moisten it.

5. Place about 2 inches (5 cm) of moistened soil in each box.

6. On the surface of the soil in each box, place one of each test material. Spread the materials so that they do not touch each other.

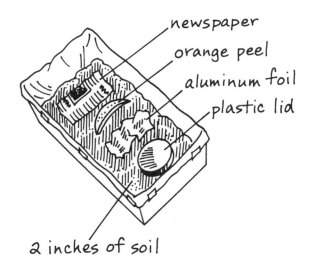

7. Fill each box with soil to cover the test materials.

8. Place the boxes in a sunny place. For the next 28 days, keep the soil in each box moist by adding equal amounts of water to each. Treat the boxes exactly the same.

9. After the first 14 days, carefully uncover the test materials of one box.

10. Use the magnifying lens to study the materials.

11. After 14 more days, uncover the materials of the second box.

12. Again, study the materials with the magnifying lens.

Results   After 14 days, the aluminum foil and plastic lid remain unchanged. The newspaper and orange peel show some signs of breaking down. After 28 days, the aluminum foil and plastic lid still remain unchanged, and the newspaper and orange peel show more signs of breaking down.

Why?   When garbage is thrown into a landfill, it is hoped that **microorganisms** (microscopic living organisms) in the soil will cause the materials to decompose. Some materials take longer than others to decompose. Things like paper and food substances can take only a few days, while plastics and aluminum cans are predicted to take hundreds of years, if they decompose at all. Materials that are easily broken down by microorganisms are biodegradable.

In this experiment, the box is lined with plastic. This is similar to the clay and/or thick man-made plastic used to line sanitary landfills. Just as the plastic inside the box prevents the box from being damaged by the moist soil, the landfill liner prevents harmful **fluids** (gases and liquids) from leaking into groundwater.

Solutions to Exercises

1a. *Think!*

- What is the tallest bar on the graph?

  Most garbage is buried in landfills.

 b. *Think!*

- Which bar is as high as the 13 percent mark?

  Only 13 percent of most garbage is recycled.

2. *Think!*

- What is the largest division on the bag?

  More paper is thrown out than any other material.

23
Reusable

Learning about Renewable Energy Sources

What You Need to Know

As the population of the earth increases, the demand for energy increases. Evidence suggests that the amount of fossil fuels being used for energy is much greater than the rate at which they are being formed by nature. Too many people are using too much energy, and the fossil fuels are being used up.

Since fossil fuels are limited and nonrenewable, we must conserve what we use and conduct further research into the use of available renewable energy sources, such as geothermal, water, wind, nuclear, and solar energy.

Geothermal energy is heat energy from within the earth. When groundwater deep within the earth's crust comes into contact with **magma** (molten, or melted, rock within the earth), it can turn into steam. Geysers are an example of geothermal energy being released at the earth's surface. If the steam is trapped, a well can be drilled and the steam directed toward the blades of machines called steam turbines. These spinning turbines produce electricity. Geothermal energy is a clean source of energy. Unfortunately, there are only a few places where geothermal energy is available, and we don't know enough about the effect on the earth of removing large amounts of geothermal energy.

Nuclear energy is produced from changes in atomic **nuclei** (the heavy centers of atoms). These changes produce heat, which is used to heat water for steam to turn turbines that generate electricity. The advantage of using nuclear energy is that a small amount of fuel produces a large amount of useful energy. Another plus is that no polluting gases are produced to damage the environment. The disadvantages of using nuclear energy are that nuclear waste and nuclear reactors can be dangerous.

The sun radiates solar energy in the form of heat and light. Solar energy that reaches the earth warms its surface and the air around it. Solar energy captured by plants provides all the world's food energy. Solar energy can be active or passive. An example of active solar energy is the use of solar panels that convert solar energy to electricity. An example of passive solar energy is the use of glass in a greenhouse to allow in more solar energy. Solar energy is clean and nonpolluting, but active solar

energy is not widely used because it is expensive and does not work on cloudy days.

Water energy (energy from moving water) and **wind energy** (energy from moving air) are two of the oldest energy sources. Both are used to produce electricity. These resources cannot be used up and do not produce air pollutants, but they do have disadvantages. Harnessing water's energy requires that the environment be changed to build dams. This can affect the fish and wildlife in the area of the dam. The main drawback to wind energy is that the wind does not blow all the time.

Exercises

Use the time line to answer the following:

1. In the 1600s, what device did the Europeans experiment with to protect tropical plants brought home by explorers?

2. The first hydrogenerating (water energy) power plant in the United States was built in Wisconsin. What date was it built?

3. The first commercial nuclear reactor was built in Pennsylvania. What date was it built?

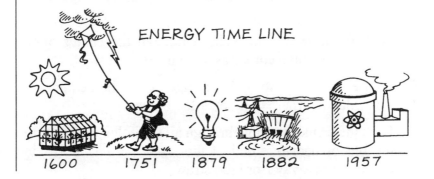

ENERGY TIME LINE

| 1600 | 1751 | 1879 | 1882 | 1957 |

Activity: WIND POWER

Purpose To show how wind can be used to perform work.

Materials scissors
ruler
typing paper
thick pencil
coin
paper hole-punch
drinking straw
modeling clay
cardboard tube from a roll of paper towels
masking tape
thread
paper clip
fan

Procedure

1. Cut a 6-by-6-inch (15-by-15-cm) square from the paper.

2. Draw two diagonal lines across the paper square so that you have an X.

3. Use the coin to draw a circle in the center of the paper.

4. Cut along the four diagonal lines up to the edge of the circle.

5. With the hole-punch, make a hole in the center of the circle and at each corner as shown.

6. Fold each corner so its hole aligns over the center hole. The folded corners will be called blades.

7. Push the drinking straw through all the holes, and position the blades near one end of the straw so that the folded corners face away from the straw.

8. Wrap a small piece of clay around both sides of the straw next to the blades to keep them in place.

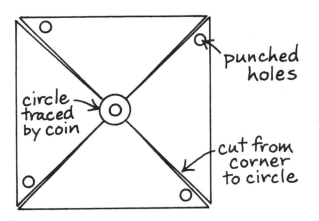

9. With the hole-punch, make two holes opposite each other near one end of the cardboard tube.

10. Insert the pencil in the holes in the tube and move the pencil around to make the holes slightly larger than the straw.

11. Tape the other end of the tube near the edge of a table.

12. Insert the free end of the straw through the holes in the tube so that the blades face the center of the table.

13. Cut a 2-foot (60-cm) piece of thread.

14. Tape one end of the thread about 2 inches (5 cm) from the end of the straw.

15. Tie the paper clip to the free end of the thread.

16. Place a fan about 1 foot (30 cm) in front of the blades.

17. Turn the fan on low speed.

18. Observe the movement of the blades, straw, and paper clip.

Results   The blades and the straw turn. The string winds around the turning straw, lifting the paper clip.

Why?   The paper blades are a model of a simple machine called a wheel and axle. This machine, which consists of a large

wheel to which a smaller wheel or axle is attached, is used to lift objects. The model demonstrates how a windmill works.

The wind from the fan hits against the model windmill's blades (the wheel), turning them around. The wheel turns in a large circle, making the straw (the axle) turn in a smaller circle. As the wheel makes one large turn, the string winds once around the turning axle. The model windmill, like real windmills, harnesses the energy of wind to perform work. Windmills can be used to pump water, grind grain, or produce electricity.

Solutions to Exercises

1. *Think!*

- Find 1600 on the time line.

- What development corresponds with this date?

  The Europeans first experimented with the greenhouse, a form of passive solar energy.

2. *Think!*

- Find the hydrogenerating power plant on the time line.
- What date corresponds with this development?

  The first hydrogenerating power plant was built in Wisconsin in 1882.

3. *Think!*

- Find the nuclear reactor on the time line.
- What date corresponds with this development?

  The first commercial nuclear reactor was built in Pennsylvania in 1957.

24
Limited

How Farmers and Ranchers Produce Food While Protecting the Earth's Limited Natural Resources

What You Need to Know

Agriculture is the science of producing healthy plants and animals for food, clothing, paper, medicines, cosmetics, and many other products. Water and soil are the two most important resources that an **agriculturist** (an expert in agriculture, such as a farmer or rancher) needs. These resources are limited, but if properly managed, they are reusable.

Agriculturists carefully manage soil to grow healthy plants and animals. Four examples of soil management are the following:

1. **Contour farming:** On steep hillsides, crops are planted across the hill instead of up and down the hill. This prevents soil erosion by water.

2. **Crop rotation:** Some crops need different nutrients from the soil. Planting different crops each season gives the soil time to renew itself.

3. **Drip irrigation:** By releasing water directly on the base of plants, less water is wasted.

4. **Windbreaks:** Planting trees and shrubs protects fields from wind and stops soil erosion.

Agriculturists do many things to help the environment. They reseed trees in forests where trees are cut for paper and wood products. They also maintain forests and grasslands, which provide food and shelter for much of the nation's wildlife.

New and old ways are being used to properly maintain the land without harming the environment. Natural predators such as ladybugs can be used to kill unwanted pests that destroy crops. Scientists are working to develop plants that are more resistant to insects. Computers are being used to run planting and harvesting equipment and even to help manage the feeding and care of animals. You may be the future scientist who produces or improves on new products, such as road deicers (materials that melt snow and ice) made from corn, fuels made from grain, or biodegradable plastics made from farm products.

Exercises

1. Unscramble these words, which are used by agriculturists:

   wiknbdare
   oruoctn ngafmri
   egairtluruc

2. Match each unscrambled word with the figure that represents it.

Activity: SMALL PORTION

Purpose To demonstrate the amount of land available for agriculture.

Material red, blue, yellow, and green modeling clay
knife (to be used only by an adult)
adult helper

Procedure

1. Shape a piece of the red clay into a ball about the size of an apple.

2. Ask an adult to cut a ¼ section from the ball.

3. Cover the curved surface of the ¾ section with blue clay.

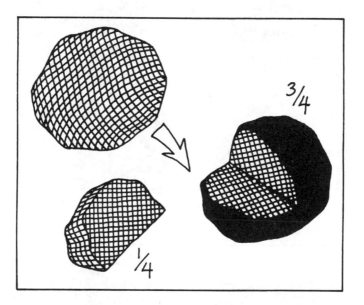

4. Cover the curved surface of the ¼ section with yellow clay.

5. Ask an adult to help cut the ¼ section in half lengthwise to make two ⅛ sections.

6. Ask an adult to cut one of the ⅛ sections into four equal parts to make four ⅟₃₂ sections.

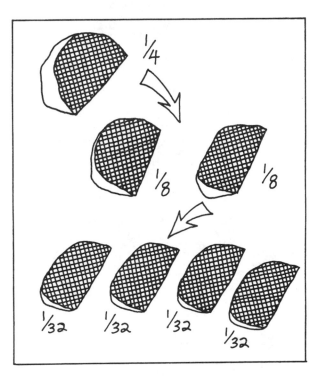

7. Cover the curved surface of one of the ⅟₃₂ sections with green clay.

Results   The red clay ball is cut into six separate pieces and the curved surfaces are covered with different colors of clay. One curved surface is blue, four are yellow, and one is green. All the flat surfaces remain red.

Why?   The red ball represents the earth. The ¾ section covered in blue represents the area of the earth covered by oceans. The yellow ⅛ section represents land areas such as the Antarctic, deserts, mountains, and swamps, where no crops can be grown. The three yellow ⅟₃₂ sections represent land areas that are too wet, too hot, or too rocky, or that have soil that is too

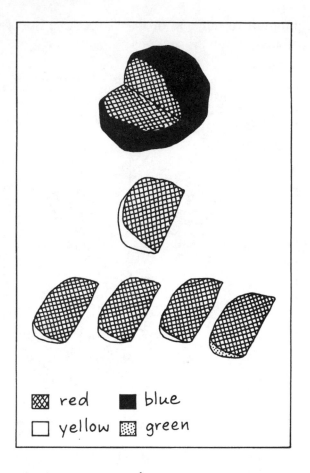

poor for agriculture. The last $\frac{1}{32}$ section, covered in green, represents the land area where all food and other agricultural products are produced.

Solutions to Exercises

1.   *Think!*

wiknbdare   WINDBREAK
oruoctn ngafmri   CONTOUR FARMING
egairtluruc   AGRICULTURE

The unscrambled words are windbreak, contour farming, and agriculture.

2a. *Think!*

- The crops are planted around a hill.

  Figure A represents contour farming.

b. *Think!*

- Animals and plants are grown for food and other uses.

  Figure B represents agriculture.

c. *Think!*

- Trees planted near a planted field protect the field from wind.

  Figure C represents a windbreak.

25
Endangered

Learning about Endangered Animals

What You Need to Know

Extinction is the dying out of a species of any living thing. It is the complete disappearance of a species from the earth, forever. Animals that are **endangered** are those in immediate danger of becoming extinct if something isn't done soon to save them.

Fossils, which are the remains of prehistoric animals and plants, show that extinctions have occurred throughout earth's history. Natural disasters, such as volcanic eruptions or changes in the climate, cause extinctions. Organisms that cannot adapt to the changes die.

A mass (large-scale) extinction occurred about 65 million years ago, when the dinosaurs died out. One current theory is that a meteorite collided with the earth, creating a cloud of dust that encircled the earth for several years. The cloud blocked the sun's light and caused temperatures to fall, resulting in the death of many kinds of plants and animals.

Extinction has been occurring naturally for millions of years, and it continues to do so. The current problem is that species are becoming extinct because of humans. One reason is that there are more people on the earth every day. More people require more space to live in and more natural resources, such as water, lumber, minerals, oil, and other products from the land. Other organisms have to compete with people for space and natural resources. People usually win.

Another way humans are endangering animals is by changing the environment. Each species has special adaptations suited to its habitat. If this habitat is quickly changed, the organism may not be able to adapt, and so it dies. Look around your neighborhood. The buildings for houses and stores and the parking lots and streets cover land that was once the home of plants and animals. During the construction of these buildings and roads, the animals moved to a different location, but if they were not able to find food and shelter, they died. The building of one neighborhood does not cause the extinction of a species unless it is the only place on earth in which the species exists. However, the building of many neighborhoods could cause species to become endangered or extinct.

Extinction can also come about because of pollution. Again, the source of this problem can be people. Examples of man-made pollutants that are endangering animals are as follows:

- Pesticides are used to get rid of "pest" species, but the poison often harms more than just the pest.

- Chemicals dumped into waterways not only affect drinking water supplies for people, but can also poison birds, fish, plants, and other life-forms, as well as the animals that eat these organisms.

- Oil spills in both fresh and marine environments threaten, and have long-lasting effects on, the lives of many species. Oil can suffocate and poison marine life. It can also cause fish not to hatch from their eggs or to be deformed.

- Polluting gases from the burning of fossil fuels affect all living organisms. See Chapter 20, "Acid Rain," for more information about the effects of air pollution.

- Waste that finds its way into oceans, lakes, and ponds can be mistaken by animals as food. Plastic and other waste items can be deadly to animals.

Some of the animals that are on the endangered species list are big cats (such as the cheetah), alligators, eastern gray kangaroos, whales, egrets, birds of paradise, burrowing owls, and many different species of fish.

Is the answer to stop building homes, offices, shopping centers, and roads or to stop driving cars? No, but changes can be and are being made. One way people are helping is by setting aside natural habitats in the form of meadow reserves in city parks, wildlife refuges, and reserves.

Another way to help would be to reduce the use of damaging chemical pollutants or to use replacements that serve the same purpose. Air pollution is reduced when people ride buses or carpool. Pesky garden insects can be kept under control by natural means instead of with dangerous chemicals. For example, chives planted around a rosebush can protect the rose from some insects that attack it.

Many of the solutions are adult decisions. But what can you do? When you visit natural reserves, don't pick the plants. Place your waste in designated containers, and walk on prepared paths. Remember, you are a visitor. Leave the area as you found it.

Exercises

1. According to the Population Growth bar graph, how many more people are estimated to inhabit the earth by the year 2000 than lived in 1650?

2. The rate of extinction is directly linked to population. According to the bar graph, between what dates will the greatest number of species most likely become extinct?

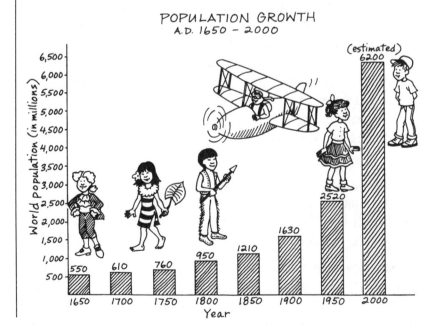

POPULATION GROWTH
A.D. 1650 – 2000

Activity: TOO MUCH, TOO FAST

Purpose   To demonstrate the effect of overfishing.

Materials   scissors
    2 dishwashing sponges
    large bowl
    tap water
    small tea strainer
    small bowl
    large tea strainer
    helper

Procedure

1. Cut each sponge into 1-inch (2.5-cm) cubes.

2. Fill the large bowl with water.

3. Place 10 sponge cubes in the water, spreading the cubes over the water's surface.

4. Ask your helper to close his or her eyes and move the small strainer through the water once to scoop up as many cubes as possible.

5. Remove the cubes from the strainer and place them in the small bowl.

6. Count the number of cubes remaining in the water, and add an equal number of cubes to double the amount of cubes in the water.

7. Repeat steps 4 to 6 three times. On the last scooping, do not add any cubes.

8. Start over with 10 cubes in the water.

9. Ask your helper to do steps 4 and 5 four times using the large strainer. After the last time, count the cubes remaining in the water and add an equal number of cubes to double the amount of cubes in the water.

Results   The number of cubes in the bowl increases when the small strainer was used and cubes were added after each scooping. The number of cubes greatly decreases and may even be zero after four scoops with the large strainer.

Why?   The sponge cubes represent fish and the strainers commercial fishing nets. Scooping with the small strainer is like fishing with fewer nets and catching fewer fish. Adding cubes represents reproduction of fish. With a need to provide fish to feed the growing human population, commercial fishing boats haul in more fish. Large catches are a problem when the fish that are left cannot lay their eggs fast enough to keep up. Overfishing removes fish faster than they can reproduce as demonstrated by using the large strainer and not adding cubes after each scooping. Some fish are in danger of becoming extinct because of overfishing.

Solutions to Exercises

1. *Think!*

- What is the estimated population of the earth for the year 2000? 6,200 million.

- What was the population in 1650? It was 550 million.

- What is the difference between these numbers?

  6,200 million – 550 million = ?

  By the year 2000, 5,650 million more people will inhabit the earth than lived in 1650.

2. *Think!*

- Between what dates does the population change the most?

  More species are likely to become extinct between 1950 and 2000.

Glossary

abiotic: Nonliving.

acid: A solution that has a pH less than 7; also a solution having this pH value.

acid rain: Any kind of precipitation that is acid.

adaptation: A physical characteristic or behavior that allows an organism to adjust to the conditions of a particular environment.

agriculture: The science of producing healthy plants and animals for food and other uses.

agriculturist: An expert in agriculture, such as a farmer or rancher.

algae: Simple plantlike organisms found in water or on wet surfaces.

Antarctic Circle: The imaginary boundary of the southern polar region.

Arctic Circle: The imaginary boundary of the northern polar region.

atmosphere: The layer of air surrounding the earth.

atom: One of the tiny particles of which all things are made.

base: A solution that has a pH greater than 7; capable of reducing the amount of acid in a substance.

benthos: Animals, such as clams, and plants, such as kelp, that live on the bottom of the ocean regardless of water depth. Most plants live in shallow water.

biodegradable: Able to be broken down into nonharmful substances by the action of living organisms, especially bacteria.

biome: An ecosystem that covers a large geographic area where plants of one type live due to the specific climate in the area.

biosphere: The living part of the planet consisting of a thin layer that extends from just above to just below the earth's surface. The combined ecosystems of the earth.

biotic: Living.

canopy layer: A forest's second layer, or roof. Consists of a network of branches and leaves, forms a covering that blocks some of the sunlight from lower plants.

carbon dioxide: A gas found in air that is used in photosynthesis and produced by respiration; one of the greenhouse gases.

carnivores: Animals that eat other animals.

cellulose: Plant fiber.

CFCs: Chlorofluorocarbon gases that are released into the atmosphere as air pollutants and that change ozone to oxygen in the ozone layer.

chlorophyll: A green light-absorbing pigment used in photosynthesis.

climate: An area's weather over an extended period of time.

cloven hooves: Split hooves.

cold desert: A desert with daytime temperatures below freezing for part of the year.

colonial animals: Animals that live in colonies.

colony: A large population whose members depend on each other.

commensalism: A relationship in which a guest organism lives on or in a host organism. The guest organism benefits from the relationship, but the host is neither helped nor harmed.

community: A group of different populations.

condensation: The process by which a gas, such as water vapor, changes to a liquid when cooled; also the water that results from this process.

condense: To change from a gas to a liquid as a result of being cooled.

coniferous forest: A forest containing coniferous plants and existing where winters are very cold, summers are brief, and rainfall is low, such as in the northern parts of North America, Europe, and Asia, and in the world's mountain regions. Also called a boreal forest, northern coniferous forest, or taiga.

coniferous plant: A plant, usually an evergreen, whose seeds are produced in cones and that typically has needles instead of leaves.

conserve: To protect from waste or destruction.

consumers: Organisms (specifically, animals) that are not able to produce their own food and must eat other organisms.

contour farming: The practice of planting crops across a hill rather than up and down the hill to prevent soil erosion by water.

coral: Live coral is made of polyps. Dead coral is a hard, stony substance made up of the skeletons of polyps.

crop rotation: The practice of planting different crops each season so that the soil has time to renew itself.

deciduous forest: A forest containing deciduous plants and existing where temperatures are mild and rainfall is abundant.

deciduous plant: A plant that sheds all or nearly all its leaves each year.

decompose: To rot or decay as a result of being broken down by microorganisms.

decomposers: Organisms such as bacteria and fungi that decompose dead plants and animals.

deforestation: The stripping away of trees.

desert: A land area that receives less than 10 inches (25 cm) of precipitation a year, that loses more water through evaporation than it gains from precipitation, and that has high summer temperatures.

dilute: To lessen the strength of a material by mixing it with another material, usually water.

dirty fallout: Air pollutants dropped by prevailing winds.

disperse: To spread to another location.

dormant: Inactive.

drip irrigation: The practice of spraying water directly on the base of plants so that less water is needed to help them grow.

drought: An extended period of unusually low rainfall.

dry deposits: Air pollutants that quickly fall to the ground without combining with moisture.

ecological community: The interaction of living organisms with their environment.

ecologist: A scientist who studies organisms and their environment.

ecology: The study of living things in their environment.

ecosystem: A distinct area that combines biotic communities and the abiotic environments with which they interact.

ecotone: The area where two or more ecosystems merge.

elevation: The height above sea level.

emergent layer: A forest's upper layer, produced by the tallest trees.

endangered: In immediate danger of becoming extinct.

environment: The natural surroundings of an organism, which include everything, living and nonliving, that affects the organism.

ephemeral: An organism that has a short life cycle.

epiphyte: A plant that grows on another plant in a relationship of commensalism.

equator: The imaginary boundary that divides the earth in half north and south.

estivate: To spend the summer in a sleeplike condition of partial or total inactivity.

evaporate: To change from a liquid to a gas as a result of being heated.

evergreen: A plant whose needles or leaves remain green throughout the year.

extinction: The dying out of a species of any living thing; the complete disappearance of a species from the earth, forever.

fauna: All the animals in a particular area.

fertilize: To join male sperm with a female egg.

first-order consumers: Animals that eat plants.

floor layer: A forest's sixth and bottom layer, made up of lichens and mosses growing in the remains of fallen trees, branches, and leaves.

flora: All the plants in a particular area.

fluid: Matter in a gas or liquid state.

food chain: A series of organisms linked together in the order in which they feed on each other.

food web: All of the interlinked food chains in a community or an ecosystem.

forest: A biome whose main vegetation consists of large groups of trees that usually grow close enough together that their tops touch, shading the ground.

fossil fuel: Any deposit of fossil materials, such as petroleum, natural gas, or coal, that can be burned to produce energy.

fossils: Traces of the remains of prehistoric animals and plants.

geothermal energy: Heat energy from within the earth.

grassland: A biome whose main vegetation is grass or grasslike plants.

greenhouse: A structure, usually made of glass or clear plastic, that provides a protected, controlled environment for raising plants indoors.

greenhouse effect: The warming of the earth by greenhouse gases.

greenhouse gases: Atmospheric gases, mostly carbon dioxide and water vapor, that trap the warmth from the sun, just as glass traps warmth in a greenhouse.

guest: Organism living on or in a host; a parasite.

habitat: The physical place, such as a desert, forest, or single tree, where a plant or animal lives and which is usually described by its physical features; also the natural home of a community.

herbivores: Animals that eat only plants; first-order consumers.

herb layer: A forest's fifth layer, found close to the ground and containing plants such as flowers, grasses, ferns, seedling trees, and shrubs.

hibernate: To spend the winter in a sleeplike condition of partial or total inactivity.

host: An organism on or in which a parasite lives and whose support of the parasite often leads to its own injury.

hot desert: A desert with hot daytime temperatures for most of the year.

incinerate: To burn to ashes.

insolation: The amount of solar energy that reaches the earth.

insulator: A material that does not easily gain or lose energy.

kelp: Underwater forests of tall, brown algae that grow in cool coastal waters.

leachate: A mixture of rainwater and other liquids that comes from garbage.

lichen: A combination of two organisms, fungus and green algae, that live in a relationship of mutualism.

magma: Molten, or melted, rock within the earth.

marine life: Plants and animals of the ocean.

microorganisms: Living organisms so small they can only be seen through a microscope.

midnight zone: The area of the ocean beneath the twilight zone, extending from 3,000 feet (1,000 m) down to the ocean floor, where only about 1 percent of marine life can survive.

migrate: To move from one place to another.

molecule: The smallest part of a substance that has all the characteristics of the substance.

mountain: A biome of high ground with various types of vegetation depending on the elevation.

mutualism: A relationship in which two organisms of two different species live together and both organisms receive some benefit.

nekton: Animals, such as fish and whales, that move independently of water currents between the bottom and surface of the ocean.

neutral: Having a pH of 7 and thus being neither acidic nor basic.

niche: The location and role or job for which a species is well suited within its community, including its habitat, what it eats, its activities, and its interaction with other living things.

node: Where leaves grow from a plant stem.

Northern Hemisphere: The area of the earth above the equator.

northern temperate zone: The region between latitudes 23.5°N and 66.5°N.

nuclear energy: Energy produced from changes in atomic nuclei.

nuclei: The heavy centers of atoms.

oceans: The largest bodies of water on earth.

omnivores: Animals that eat both plants and animals.

organisms: All living things, including people, plants, animals, bacteria, and fungi.

oxygen: An atmospheric gas made up of two oxygen atoms that is necessary for respiration. Its symbol is O_2.

oxygen cycle: The recycling of oxygen-containing gases between plants and animals.

ozone: A form of oxygen made up of three oxygen atoms that forms the ozone layer. Its symbol is O_3.

ozone cycle: The ongoing process by which ozone breaks down and re-forms in the ozone layer.

ozone layer: Scattered molecules of ozone gas that collect in the upper atmosphere of the earth in a layer that shields the earth from excessive ultraviolet light.

parasite: An organism that lives on or in a host organism and that gets its food from or at the expense of its host.

parasitism: A relationship in which one organism, a parasite, secures its nourishment by living on or inside a host organism at the expense of its host.

permafrost: A layer of permanently frozen soil underground. An important feature of a tundra.

pH: The unit of measure for determining whether a solution is acidic, basic, or neutral.

pH scale: The scale, ranging from 0 to 14, used to measure the pH of a solution.

photosynthesis: The process by which plants use light energy trapped by chlorophyll to change carbon dioxide and water into food.

phytoplankton: Plant plankton.

plankton: Small to microscopic organisms that live near the ocean's surface and are carried along by the currents. Animal plankton are called **zooplankton**, and plant plankton are called **phytoplankton**.

pollutants: Substances that destroy the purity of air, water, or land.

polyp: A tiny, tubelike marine animal of which live coral is made, one end of which is attached to the sea bottom, to rocks, or to one another and the opposite end of which is a mouth surrounded by fingerlike, stinging tentacles.

population: Organisms of the same species living together in a specific area; also the total count of individuals in a specific area, such as the population of a town.

precipitation: Water that returns to the earth as rain, hail, sleet, or snow.

predator: An animal that hunts and kills other animals for food.

prevailing winds: Winds that blow consistently from one direction.

producers: Organisms (specifically, plants) that can produce their own food.

rebus: Pictures and symbols used to represent a word.

recycle: To use again.

respiration: An ongoing process by which plants and animals take in oxygen and give out carbon dioxide.

sanitary landfill: A solid waste disposal area that protects the environment from leachate.

scrub: Plants, such as small trees and shrubs, that usually have many stems, unlike trees which have one main trunk.

sea level: The level of the surface of the ocean.

second-order consumers: Animals that eat first-order consumers.

semiarid: Having a climate that is dry, but not as dry as a desert.

shrub layer: A forest's fourth layer, made of shrubs.

snow line: The height on a mountain above which snow stays year-round.

social group: A small population that lives and travels together and in some ways depends on each other for its well-being.

soil erosion: The wearing away of the soil by wind or water.

solar energy: Energy from the sun.

solution: A mixture made by dissolving a substance in a liquid, such as water.

Southern Hemisphere: The area of the earth below the equator.

southern temperate zone: The region between latitudes 23.5°S and 66.5°S.

species: A group of similar and related organisms.

stomata: Tiny pores on the surface of plant leaves that can open and close to take in and give out water vapor.

subcanopy layer: A forest's third layer, formed by the leaves and branches of shorter trees under the canopy layer.

succulent plants: Plants that have thick, fleshy leaves or stems for storing water.

sunlight zone: The upper 488 feet (150 m) of the ocean, where sunlight penetrates and where about 90 percent of all marine life live.

superorganism: An organism, such as coral or the Portuguese man-of-war, that appears to be one organism, but in fact is a number of colonial animals joined together.

third-order consumers: Animals that eat first- and/or second-order consumers.

top consumer: An organism at the top of a food chain.

transpiration: The loss of water into the atmosphere through the stomata of plants.

tree line: The height on a mountain above which the climate is too cold for trees to grow.

tropical rain forest: A forest that gains more water from precipitation than it loses through evaporation. Located in the tropical zone and having an average temperature between 70° and 85°F (21° and 29°C) and average yearly rainfall of more than 80 inches (200 cm).

tropical zone: The region between latitudes 23.5°S and 23.5°N.

tundra: A treeless biome mainly in the north polar areas that has long frigid winters and brief summers and where grasses, mosses, lichen, low shrubs, and a few flowering plants survive.

twilight zone: The shadowy area of the ocean, extending from the bottom of the sunlight zone down to about 3,000 feet (1,000 m), where plants cannot grow and where animals are less numerous and smaller.

ultraviolet (UV) light: High-energy rays of sunlight.

vegetation: Plant life.

water cycle: The recycling of water between the earth and the atmosphere.

water energy: Energy from moving water.

water vapor: The gas state of water.

weed: Any plant that grows where it is not wanted.

wet deposits: Air pollutants that mix with moisture in the air before falling to the ground.

wildflower: A flowering plant that grows in woods, deserts, or other natural areas.

windbreaks: The practice of planting trees and shrubs to protect fields from soil erosion by wind.

wind energy: Energy from moving air.

zooplankton: Animal plankton.

Index

Get these fun and exciting books by Janice VanCleave
at your local bookstore, call toll-free 1-800-225-5945, or
fill out the order form below and mail to:
John Wiley & Sons, Inc., Order Processing Department,
432 Elizabeth Ave.
Somerset, New Jersey 08875

Visit our Website at:
www.wiley.com

Janice VanCleave's Science Fair for Every Kid Series

__Astronomy	53573-7	$12.95 US / $19.95 CAN
__Biology	50381-9	$11.95 US / $17.95 CAN
__Chemistry	62085-8	$12.95 US / $19.95 CAN
__Constellations	15979-4	$12.95 US / $19.95 CAN
__ Dinosaurs	30812-9	$10.95 US / $16.95 CAN
__Earth Science	53010-7	$12.95 US / $19.95 CAN
__Ecology	10086-2	$10.95 US / $16.95 CAN
__ Food/ Nutrition	17665-6	$12.95 US / $19.95 CAN
__Geography	59842-9	$12.95 US / $19.95 CAN
__ Geometry	31141-3	$12.95 US / $19.95 CAN
__Human Body	02408-2	$12.95 US / $19.95 CAN
__ Math	54265-2	$12.95 US / $19.95 CAN
__ Oceans	12453-2	$12.95 US / $19.95 CAN
__ Physics	52505-7	$12.95 US / $19.95 CAN

Janice VanCleave's Spectacular Science Projects

__Animals	55052-3	$10.95 US / $16.95 CAN
__Earthquakes	57107-5	$10.95 US / $16.95 CAN
__Electricity	31010-7	$10.95 US / $16.95 CAN
__Gravity	55050-7	$10.95 US / $16.95 CAN
__Insects/Spiders	16396-1	$10.95 US / $16.95 CAN
__Machines	57108-3	$10.95 US / $16.95 CAN
__Magnets	57106-7	$10.95 US / $16.95 CAN
__Microscopes & Magnifying Lenses	58956-X	$10.95 US / $16.95 CAN
__Molecules	55054-X	$10.95 US / $16.95 CAN
__Plants	14687-0	$10.95 US / $16.95 CAN
__Rocks and Minerals	10269-5	$10.95 US / $16.95 CAN
__Solar System	32204-0	$10.95 US / $16.95 CAN
__Volcanoes	30811-0	$10.95 US / $16.95 CAN
__Weather	03231-X	$10.95 US / $16.95 CAN

Janice VanCleave's Science Bonanzas

__200 Gooey, Slippery, Slimy, Weird & Fun Experiments
57921-1 $12.95 US / $19.95 CAN
__201 Awesome, Magical, Bizarre, & Incredible Experiments
31011-5 $12.95 US / $19.95 CAN
__202 Oozing, Bubbling, Dripping & Bouncing Experiments
14025-2 $12.95 US / $19.95 CAN
__203 Icy, Freezing, Frosty, Cool & Wild Experiments
25223-9 $12.95 US / $19.95 CAN

Janice VanCleave's A+ Projects Series

__Biology	58628-5	$12.95 US / $19.95 CAN
__Chemistry	58630-7	$12.95 US / $19.95 CAN
__Earth Science	17770-9	$12.95 US / $19.95 CAN

Prices Subject to Change

WILEY
Independent Thinkers